LOOK BEHIND YOU

LOOK BEHIND YOU

by Daniel Wain

JOSEF WEINBERGER PLAYS

LONDON

Look Behind You
First published in 2001
by Josef Weinberger Ltd
12-14 Mortimer Street, London, W1T 3JJ

ISBN 0 85676 241 5

Printed by Commercial Colour Press, London E7

Dedicated with everlasting love,
admiration and gratitude to my sister, Jo –
the antithesis of luvvie-dom,
and my greatest friend

LOOK BEHIND YOU was first presented by Strut & Fret Theatre Company at The Tabard Theatre, London, on 24th November 1999, with the following cast, in order of appearance:

ANASTASIA KRABBE / FAIRY BOWBELLS	Cait Chidgey
NORMA BAILEY / QUEEN RAT	Katharine Waugh
MAGGIE DUNN	Tracy Jewitt
WENDY WESTCOTT-HALL / TOMMY	Julie Mayhew
NICHOLAS MAY / IDLE JACK	Piers Garnham
SALLY MUSTO / ALICE FITZWARREN	Florence May Whitaker
SUZANNE BRETT / CHORUS MEMBER	Maxime V Allan
ROBIN ELDRIDGE / ALDERMAN FITZWARREN	Simon Stanhope
JAKE CAFFREY / DICK WHITTINGTON	Ben Garcia
BERNIE BIGELOW / CAPTAIN BARNACLE	Neil Fletcher
TOM NANCARROW / SARAH THE COOK	Daniel Wain

Directed by Marc Brenner
Designed by Richard Evans
Stage Managed by Dan Rainsford
Assisted by Flavia Fraser-Cannon and Josey Grimshaw
Costumes by Phil Newman
Scenic Artistry by Lisa Davis and Minnie MacDonald
Props by Ingrid Holtz and Matthew Wilson

Produced by Daniel Wain

The main action of LOOK BEHIND YOU takes place backstage during performances of *Dick Whittington* between 16th December (opening night) and 23rd January (last night). The extracts of *Dick Whittington* take place during any performance between those two dates.

More than the 'big events', the agonies and the ecstasies, the traumas and the triumphs, it is the choice that we make about the way we conduct ourselves every day that determines the quality of our lives – DW

AUTHOR'S NOTES

A NOTE ON THE SPEECH LAYOUT AND OVERLAPPING DIALOGUE

A speech / line normally follows the one immediately preceding it. However:

When one character starts to speak before the other has finished, the interruption point is marked with a hash (#). For example:

MAGGIE   And there do need to be rules, for everyone's #
            sake . . .

JAKE   You're queen.

Here, JAKE takes as his cue the end of the word "everyone's", so that he begins his line at the same time as MAGGIE continues to say the word "sake".

This means that occasionally a character continues to speak right through another's speech:

ANASTASIA   If you like playing in mortuaries! # Next scene,

NORMA   Oh, but, well . . .

ANASTASIA   I am taking a mirror on.

Here, ANASTASIA says the line "Next scene, I am taking a mirror on" without pause, with NORMA saying "Oh, but, well . . ." underneath her, her cue being after the word "mortuaries". (NB: If there had been a full stop after ANASTASIA's "Next scene", she would have waited until NORMA had said "well" before continuing with "I am taking a mirror on".)

If a speech follows on from a speech earlier than the one immediately before it, the continuity is marked with an asterisk (*). For example:

SUZANNE   Oh, Jake, just in time. Can you unzip me? *

JAKE   Well, I'll do my best.

MAGGIE   * Can't someone else do that somewhere else?

Here, the end of SUZANNE's line is the cue for both JAKE and MAGGIE to start speaking.

Occasionally, some of the above are combined. However, provided the principles are followed, all should be well!

SUZANNE   I'm ready for some of this trusting, Nick. Are
                you? # Or is

SALLY   Focus. Concentration. 110 percent. *

SUZANNE   that only important on stage?

NICK   (*to* SUZANNE) Not now for Christ's sake!

MAGGIE   * Sally, you are going to be fine.

Here, SUZANNE speaks her lines without pausing to acknowledge SALLY's interruption. NICK therefore answers her question, "Or is that only important on stage?" immediately after she has posed it. SALLY begins speaking after SUZANNE has said "Are you?", with MAGGIE taking "110 percent" as her cue to begin speaking. Therefore the conversation between SALLY and MAGGIE begins whilst that between SUZANNE and NICK is still taking place.

The golden rule is always to aim for as 'natural' interchanges as possible, whilst ensuring that 'important' lines are not talked over.

A NOTE ON THE TOPICAL REFERENCES

I realise that a number of the references that struck a chord in late 1999, and still do in 2000, might lose topicality over time. If LOOK BEHIND YOU is fortunate enough to be performed when Camelot directors, Dame Shirley Porter and Dannii Minogue no longer raise an eyebrow of recognition, yet alone a smile, then please feel free to update. Provided the replacement gets a laugh, I'm not precious . . .

A NOTE ON THE SET

The set for Look Behind You can be as simple or as complex as
you want, or can afford, it to be. The only proviso is that the
onstage pantomime scenes are always clearly delineated from
those that take place backstage. (Otherwise confusion will
reign not only on stage, but in the audience's minds as well.)
With that one crucial point always in your mind, the staging is
intended to be extremely flexible.

In the original Strut & Fret production, the brilliant Richard
Evans created a "fine, cleverly constructed set", to quote the
press, on an absolute shoestring of a budget and in a very
cosy performance space no more than 20 feet square. A central, manually operated revolve flicked the action from backstage to front and then back again in seconds. This consisted
of a simple panto flat on one side and a mock corridor wall,
with bench, payphone, theatrical posters and backstage no-
tices, on the other. The 'panto' side was so designed that flats
signifying different locations (the Stores, the *Saucy Sal*, etc)
could be swapped in the real backstage darkness whilst 'backstage' scenes were being played onstage.

The revolve aside, the only other pieces of set were black
drapes and masks either side of this central flat that formed
entrances for both backstage and frontstage scenes, and two
pieces of simple 'kit' downstage right and left respectively:
one a stage manager's desk, signifying prompt corner (ie, stage
left of the 'offstage' *Dick Whittington* stage), the other a
dressing table, with practical mirror lights, indicating a generic
dressing room. A neat (again manually operated) rope and
pulley device hid 'prompt corner' and 'dressing room' with
traditional red front tabs whenever the action moved onstage,
the curtains swishing across simultaneously with the revolve
turning, but this was an (albeit impressive) embellishment that
future productions need not necessarily incorporate. Provided
the basic scene obviously changes from back to frontstage, the
accessories can be hidden in some other, hopefully ingenious,
manner, or simply not lit.

Indeed, the entire transition from real to panto world could be
achieved through the imaginative use of lighting. Rich, why
didn't we think of that?!

A NOTE ON THE USE OF SONG AND DANCE

In the original Strut & Fret production at The Tabard (directed by the equally brilliant Marc Brenner), the use of song and dance was restricted to the 'Business is Booming' transitional scene in Act One, and to the finalé of 'There's No Business Like Showbusiness'. The other instances detailed in the stage directions were replaced, due to consideration of the running time, with very short musical interludes long enough to rotate the scene from panto to backstage or vice versa.

If running time is not such an issue for directors of future productions, they should feel free to reinstate the short musical numbers indicated in the script for scene 'topping and tailing' purposes. However, please note that the length of such song and dance routines should be strictly restricted so as not to impede the flow of the action: a chorus and one verse should be more than enough.

Daniel Wain, September 2000

ACT ONE

*The house lights and house music have faded. The auditorium
is dark and quiet. A short, loud burst of happy, triumphant
music: the show is about to start! The music ends on a
fanfare. Silence. In the darkened, hushed, expectant
auditorium there is suddenly a familiar noise: the slightly
muffled sound of a mobile phone ringing from within
someone's bag. A* LADY *answers, speaking quietly but
distinctly. As she continues, her hesitancy decreases, as her
volume increases.*

LADY   (*into phone*) Hello? Yes? What? I can't talk
                                                    now. Hello?
                    No, I'm just about to watch a show. (*A beat.*)
                                                    You know?
                    But how? No, wait . . . What?! Hang on a
                                                    minute . . .
                    What do you mean, you know because I'm in it?!
                    (*Beat.*) You're from the Fairy Finders Agency?
                    Well, that's sweet but nothing to do with me.
                    Oh, I am a fairy, you've made no mistake;
                    I'm on, however, a well-earned Christmas break.
                    (*Beat.*) True, I can't stop rhyming when I rabbit;
                    Even on hols, it's hard to kick the habit.
                    Still, enough about me, why did you phone?
                    (*Beat.*) I see . . . you're short of a fairy chaperone.

                    (*By this stage, the* LADY *is on the stage, before
                    the closed front tabs. She wears a headscarf
                    and mackintosh.*)

                    (*Still into phone.*) Look, I'm on centennial leave.
                    My last millennium you wouldn't believe!
                    Only this week, I woke Beauty from her nap
                    Then found the Babes in the Wood . . .
                                                    without a map!
                    Red Riding Hood's wolf I dogged yesterday
                    Before op'ning Aladdin's new take-away.
                    Then there's Jill: she still hasn't got over Jack,
                    I tell you, if I even see Humpty . . . I'll crack!!!
                    (*Beat; she listens.*) Dick? Dick Whittington?
                                                    Why didn't you say?

I'll take up your offer right away!

(*Ending her call and turning to address the audience.*)

Kids, we must help dear Dick if he's in need.
For with us on his side, he's bound to succeed.
So join me now on a time-travel ride
Back to 1377 and London's Cheapside.
Medieval England's overrun by rats.
The future's rocky; hold on to your hats!
What shall we do, kids? London's a zoo!
There are rats in the streets, the parlour, the loo . . .

(*There is a peel of thunder and a flash of lightning. Suddenly,* QUEEN RAT *appears in a spot of green light, downstage left. The* LADY *is now downstage right.*)

Then enter, Queen Rat, as if on cue . . .

QUEEN RAT   (*playing up the Shakespeare*)
If London be the food of rats, gnaw on!
(*To* FAIRY BOWBELLS, *for 'tis she.*) Thou canst
    not defeat my tribe, meddling moron . . .

BOWBELLS   (*to audience*)
Fret not, kids! There's no need to fear her:
She simply comes from an older era.
Indeed, whilst I think on't, I too must change
Else the townsfolk chorus shalt think me strange.

(*In a flash, the* LADY *hast verily vanished.*)

QUEEN RAT   (*to audience*)
Greetings, mere mortals. Heed not that fairy!
I rule London Town. Ain't that scary?
From the City to the Artistic Quarter,
I'm the Middle Ages' Dame Shirley Porter.

(*As she laughs hideously, the* LADY *re-appears, again downstage right but now as a fully costumed* FAIRY, *sans headscarf, handbag and mac. The two 'immortals' now face each other across the forestage.*)

BOWBELLS I'll warrant ye, not for long, foul Queen Rat!
I, Fairy Bowbells, wilt soon put paid to that!

QUEEN RAT Fairy, thou canst save thyself the trouble.
'Ere long the whole world, I'll have chewed to rubble.
As for your unsung, and as yet unseen, Dick,
He's nothing but a parsnip-planting hick!
Oh, for my regiment of rats 'twas fun
To ruin old Farmer Whittington.
Devouring all his grain, they never stopped
Until his bounteous crops . . . they'd cropped.
The father, now ruined and quite undone,
Sends Dick his fortune to seek in old London.
But rest assured, my rats and I shalt lose no time
In driving the lad from poverty to crime!

BOWBELLS A truce to words! Let the fight begin!

QUEEN RAT 'Tis good 'gainst evil

BOWBELLS   And good will win.

QUEEN RAT (*momentarily throw-away*) Oh, don't be naïve.
You know the case is
That my rats now hold very high places.
Par example, vicious, vile vermin I've sent
Without any disguise to Parliament!

BOWBELLS But now Whittington comes to steal thy crown
And win the love and respect of London Town.

QUEEN RAT Dost he know the rubbish he'll have begot?

BOWBELLS He just wants an audience . . .

QUEEN RAT   Give him this dozy lot!
(*to audience*) Heed my words: I won't waste
                                  time in slumber;
For Dick Whittington, I've got your number!
And my earthly vermin here beneath
Wilt see that you feel my razor sharp teeth!
So gather ye whatsits while ye may;
I'll crush them all ere break of day!

>(*She laughs in that frightfully false evil way
that stage villains do, then vanishes.*)

BOWBELLS   (*to audience*)
              Whilst the chorus strut their hose and doublets,
              I might as well rest my chosen couplets.
              If you need help, shout; I'll be but a twinkle;
              (*Indicating mobile phone.*)
              If shouting won't do, just give me a tinkle!
              So keep them peeled, kids. Pay close attention.
              Hold on to your seats. Our adventure's begun!

>(*To spirit-soaring, magical music,* FAIRY
BOWBELLS *vanishes, along with the scene.*)

Thursday 16th December – opening night

*When the lights return, which is after only a moment, we have
been transformed backstage, to the stage management /
prompt corner in the wings.* MAGGIE DUNN *and* WENDY
WESTCOTT-HALL *are discovered in a pool of light. The latter
has her face painted as a cat, although she wears stage
management blacks: T-shirt and slacks. Somewhere
bakcstage is an old-fashioned payphone.*

MAGGIE   (*in a hushed voice*) One scene down, twenty-
              eight more of the fuckers to go.

WENDY   (*ditto*) Do you still need me here, or can I go
              and put Tommy on?

MAGGIE   You've still got nine pages. Where's Keith?

WENDY   Keith?

MAGGIE   Your CSM.

WENDY   CS . . . ?

MAGGIE   (*interrupting; a well-worn speech*) Company
              Stage Manager. Who's supposed to manage
              the company whilst in the theatre, as opposed
              to myself, who is the TSM, the theatre stage

manager, who's only supposed to manage the theatre despite the company. Confused? (*Without waiting for an answer.*) I am. Utterly bewildered as to why I'm here showing you how to work an on-off switch, whilst Captain Keith has gone AWOL. I haven't seen him since he left the dress . . .

(*The pool of light has enlarged to show more of the backstage area, including* NICHOLAS MAY *and* SALLY MUSTO, *who are engaged in some extensive physical warm-ups, he coaching her. He is dressed as* IDLE JACK, *she as* ALICE FITZWARREN. *It should be noted straightaway that all of the actors are only ever seen dressed in their panto costume/s, except for* TOM *in the last scene of Act One, when he appears in street-wear.*)

WENDY   He went to find an authentic looking Moroccan rug.

MAGGIE   Did he go to North Africa to get it? (*Into her microphone that is linked to the dressing room tannoy.*) Mr Caffrey, your ten-minute call. Please note I'm spoiling you. Normally, you'll only get the five, but I know you're a little behind. (*Back to* WENDY.) All right, you better go get furred up.

WENDY   (*a bad attempt at hesitation*) Well, if you're absolutely sure . . .

MAGGIE   No, but we can't have Tommy going on all tits and no tail.

WENDY   (*ditto*) Well . . .

MAGGIE   Miss Westcott-Hall, your nine-minute call.

WENDY   Righto.

(*She dashes off, only to collide into the exertions of* NICK *and* SALLY.)

Oh, sorry.

NICK   No probs, Wend, # no probs.

MAGGIE   And mind the woodwork! Though if you trip
                over an authentic looking Moroccan rug, roll it
                out. Keith might be doing a Cleopatra.

                (WENDY *has gone to the offstage dressing
                rooms, possibly having paused to glance and
                grin at* NICK.)

NICK   (*to* SALLY) OK. That's good. You're doing
                really well. Just remember to keep the focus.

SALLY   (*Echoing*) Focus . . .

NICK   Focus. It's all about con-cen-tra # -tion.

SALLY   . . . tra-tion . . .

MAGGIE   (*into tannoy*) Mr Eldridge to the stage, please.
                In other words, Robin, get a fucking move on.

                (FAIRY BOWBELLS *and* QUEEN RAT *appear from
                the stage; the former is really* ANASTASIA
                KRABBE, *the latter* NORMA BAILEY. *Offstage,*
                ANASTASIA *is as obviously, and deliberately,
                East European as* NORMA *is Received
                Pronounciation. They cross and exit towards
                the offstage dressing rooms, totally ignoring*
                MAGGIE. *It should be noted here that all exits
                from, or entrances into, the non-panto
                backstage scenes are from or to other
                backstage areas such as the offstage dressing
                rooms, theatre corridors or 'stage right'
                wings, unless otherwise stated as being to or
                from 'the stage'.*)

NORMA   Not a bad house.

ANASTASIA   If you like playing in mortuaries! # Next scene,

NORMA   Oh, but, well . . .

ANASTASIA   I am taking a mirror on.

NORMA	A mirror?
ANASTASIA	Stick it under their noses; check the bastards are not dead.
NORMA	But, you see, they're a listening audience, # I think.
ANASTASIA	You can almost smell the press.
SALLY	(*overhearing this*) Oh, no, are the reviewers in?
ANASTASIA	I should know. I had to sit amongst them for long enough.
NORMA	Well, late curtain up first night, # it's almost a tradition.*
SALLY	Which ones?
ANASTASIA	* You would not get it in the States, my dear. Even with # the
NORMA	But they're definitely listening. Hardly a cough.
ANASTASIA	unions. Curtain up prompt, # every show.
NICK	(*to* SALLY) Don't worry about the crits. Con # -cen-trate!
NORMA	And one expects that in panto.
NICK	Focus.
NORMA	Colds . . .
ANASTASIA	Even in Australia, # cherie.
NORMA	Chills . . . Flu . . . # My lovely
ANASTASIA	Hayfever there.
NORMA	little lovely ones, martyrs to the snuffles, bless them . . . Oh, 'Hay Fever', oh yes, of course, you heard about my Judith at Pitlochry in . . . # well, it wasn't exactly an age ago . . .

ANASTASIA   No. I have never heard of Potlichry.

                   (*And* ANASTASIA *and* NORMA *have gone.*)

MAGGIE   (*into tannoy*) Robin, if I have to come up there
                   and get you, there'll be bleach in your custard
                   pies.

                   (NICK *and* SALLY *have moved on to vocal
                   warm-ups: lots of grunts and guttural
                   clearings.*)

                   (*to* NICK *and* SALLY) Excuse me, could you
                   keep it down. The shipwreck's not till Act
                   Two. Let's not confuse the kids. Most of them
                   are nicely dysfunctional as it is.

NICK   (*ignoring* MAGGIE; *to* SALLY) OK, you've got it
                   to the right pitch. Now let's just
                   (*Meaningfully.*) breathe.

MAGGIE   Oh, don't, not just on my account.

                   (NICK *and* SALLY *begin breathing exercises:
                   lots of serious looks and balletic arm
                   gestures.*)

                   (*into tannoy, this time to the lighting box*) It's
                   nothing to do with me, old cock, but you might
                   like to consider a blackout here. The chorus
                   has stopped dancing, the audience has
                   stopped clapping. Now they're just facing
                   each other, like blind daters waiting to be
                   introduced.

                   (NICK *has now got one hand on* SALLY'S
                   stomach, the other on her back.)

NICK   That's it. Good girl. Remember, from the #
                   diaphragm . . .

MAGGIE   (*into tannoy, as the sound of applause drifts
                   on from the stage*) And lo, it did work. (*To*

NICK.) You know, you are quite free to grunt
and sweat in your personal dressing room.

NICK   Except I don't have a personal dressing room.
              I have to share.

MAGGIE   Well, I'm sure if you went in and started doing
              that, you'd soon have it to yourself.

SALLY   I have an individual dressing room . . .

              (SUZANNE BRETT *bursts on from the stage,
              dressed as a townswoman. It should be
              pointed out here that whatever her costume,
              and she has quite a selection, they are all
              deliberately revealing.*)

SUZANNE   (*in a blaze*) Christ, what a balls-up! All over
              the shop!

MAGGIE   Sorry, not au fait with ballet jargon.

SUZANNE   I wouldn't mind but we're not even in
              Fitzwarren's Stores yet, # ho de-frigging ho!

MAGGIE   (*quietly to her*) I'm sorry, love, could you
              shout up a bit? I can hear you perfectly, but I
              think the old dear at the back of the circle's
              having a bit of trouble catching it all.

SUZANNE   Sorry. (*Beat.*) But . . . two weeks' rehearsal.
              What can you expect?

MAGGIE   The standard family panto, love. And by the
              way, I don't know if you noticed but the rest of
              the folk of London Town exited the other side.
              Looked a bit odd, you dashing past Ye Olde
              Beer Pump stage left.

SUZANNE   (*unashamedly smiling*) Well, you've got to
              make an impact, haven't you? Stand out.

MAGGIE   I don't think you've any problems in that
              department, # petal.

SUZANNE	I mean, it's not as if the director'll be giving any notes, unless they're by e-mail.
MAGGIE	Why?
SUZANNE	Quentin's already in Exeter holding auditions for 'The Dance of Death'.
MAGGIE	Oh, well, nice to know someone's enjoying themselves.

(SUZANNE *has begun to move towards* NICK *and* SALLY.)

(*to herself*) No Keith. No Quentin. God help this shit and all who fail in her. (*To* SALLY.) Miss Musto, stand by please. There's an expositional scene outside your father's Stores coming up. Mind you, if Robin doesn't get his finger out, you'll be expositioning out there on your own.

NICK	(*to* SALLY, *but self-reproachfully*) I haven't got you to proper performance pitch yet. Thirty minutes # isn't enough.
MAGGIE	(*into tannoy*) Robin, I'm sure I just heard Alice tell the audience her father must have died in his dressing room.
NICK	Tomorrow, Sally, I want you here in costume, ready to start by 6.30, OK?
SALLY	OK, # Nick.
NICK	We haven't even got to the trust exercises. You're going out there completely unfocused, # not 110 percent in
SUZANNE	I could do with a bit of warming-up, Nick, some trust exercises.
NICK	control of your own instrument, # it's not fair, I
SALLY	(*totally nervous*) Right . . .

NICK	apologise. Tomorrow: 6.30. Sharp. I insist.
MAGGIE	(*leading* SALLY *stagewards*) Tonight: 7.40. Now. I order.
SUZANNE	I'm ready for some of this trusting, Nick. Are you? # Or is
SALLY	(*to herself; a mantra*) Focus. Concentration. 110 percent. *
SUZANNE	that only important on stage?
NICK	(*to* SUZANNE) Not now for Christ's sake!
	(*He moves to one side and launches, with total concentration, into a painful-looking series of press-ups.* SUZANNE *takes out a strategically hidden hand-mirror and inspects her face gravely.*)
MAGGIE	* Sally, you are going to be fine. You're used to appearing in front of millions, # right?
SALLY	On television, yes, and # then only for a minute at a time . . .
MAGGIE	So what's a few hundred out there matter?
SALLY	Well . . .
MAGGIE	Look, pet, they want you to be good, and you will be. Even if you're not, they'll kid themselves that you were. You're the nation's sweetheart. One of them. So trust me, them, and yourself. OK?
	(ROBIN ELDRIDGE *enters, dressed as* ALDERMAN FITZWARREN, *and in absolutely no hurry whatsoever. It should be noted straightaway that* ROBIN *is not nearly as old as he acts.*)
SALLY	Thank you, Maggie, thank you # very much.

ROBIN   (*to* NICK, *who's still focused on his press-ups*)
               Don't know if you've noticed, love, but she's
               slipped out from under you.

MAGGIE   Robin! How kind of you to drop in. This
               young lady was about to go into the unknown
               unescorted.

ROBIN   (*to* SALLY) Don't listen to her, my dear. You
               can rely on me. Robin Eldridge is famed in the
               industry for his timing.

MAGGIE   Fashionably late. Did you not hear me on the
               tannoy?

ROBIN   Not after I switched the ruddy thing off, love.
               Couldn't concentrate on the crossword. Only
               four down and twelve # across to get.

MAGGIE   Well, do it once more, Robin, and I'm going to
               solder your knob on maximum. # Concentrate
               your mind on that.*

SUZANNE   (*moving to* SALLY, *having assured herself that
               her make-up is pretty much as it was when she
               left the dressing room five minutes ago*) Good
               luck, Sal. Not that you need it, babe.

SALLY   Thank you, Suzanne.

SUZANNE   Suzy, Sal, Suzy.

SALLY   Suzy.

ROBIN   * Maggie, love, you know how to get an old
               dog hot under the collar. And elsewhere.

NICK   (*finally getting up, his focus and
               concentration obviously shattered; to himself*)
               Jesus! It's like a Redcoats' Retirement Home.
               The Carry On Knacker's Yard. (*Pointedly, he
               leaves, towards the dressing rooms.*)

MAGGIE   What a splendid stage whisper. Must be
               something in those vocal warm-ups after all.

(*Stage whispering after* NICK.) Ten minutes, Mr May.

ROBIN (*calling after him, but with much heartier volume*) Hands off cocks, feet in socks! # (*To* SALLY, *as an apology.*) As my old dad used to say.

MAGGIE (*whispering ferociously*) Robin! Though you pretend otherwise, you're not deaf, and neither is the audience.

ROBIN Sorry, love, already in character. (*To* SALLY.) Only hope I can keep it up on the green, my dear.

SALLY The green?

MAGGIE Greengage: stage.

SALLY Oh, rhyming # slang. How cute.

MAGGIE (*pushing* ROBIN *towards the stage,* SALLY *following*) So on you go then. If you're a good boy, when you get back, I'll help you with twelve across.

SALLY (*to* MAGGIE) I won't forget what you said, about # trusting in them and in myself . . .

MAGGIE Forget it, sweetheart. Forget everything. Except your lines.

SUZANNE (*suddenly hugging* SALLY *as she heads stagewards*) Ooh, love you, Sal. Go get 'em, babe! You'll be fab, totally fab. I'm so proud!

MAGGIE (*looking stagewards; flatly*) So am I, now get on.

ROBIN (*to* SALLY, *giving her a quick peck on the cheek*) Let us go meet our adoring public. Stick by me, love.

(ROBIN *leads* SALLY *onstage; shortly there is heard a polite round of applause. It should be noted that throughout the backstage scenes,*

there is a certain limited amount of noise from
the stage and auditorium: bursts of music,
applause, laughter – just enough never to let
us forget that a show is in progress.)

MAGGIE   "Stick by me. I may need prompting." (*Beat.*)
          So, you and Sally old buddies then, or were
          you just auditioning for 'Little Women'?

SUZANNE   Actually, we met at rehearsals last week, when
          they put the chorus and principals together.
          Still, nothing wrong with a bit of theatrical
          camaraderie.

MAGGIE   No, nowt wrong at all with a bit of back-
          (*emphasising the word*) slapping. (*Beat; a*
          look.) There appears to be a 'Dick on Highgate
          Hill' scene fast approaching and, knowing this
          particular Dick, that must herald some kind of
          chorus warbling and gambolling in the
          background.

SUZANNE   So?

MAGGIE   So, shouldn't you join the other gambolling
          warblers? Or do you plan to enter over the
          grassy knoll stage left?

          (*Before* SUZANNE *can answer,* JAKE CAFFREY
          appears backstage, dressed as DICK
          WHITTINGTON.)

JAKE   Sorry I missed the warm-up.

MAGGIE   Don't worry, Mr Caffrey, it's not obligatory.
          Or indeed recommended.

SUZANNE   Oh, Jake, just in time. Can you unzip me? *

          (*She immediately turns around to enable him*
          to do so.)

JAKE   Well, I'll do my best.

MAGGIE   * Can't someone else do that somewhere
          elsewhere?

SUZANNE	(*as* JAKE *does; to* MAGGIE) The other warblers'll be too busy gambolling to stage right. (*Turning to* JAKE.) Thanks.
JAKE	No problem.
	(SUZANNE *gives him an eyelash-fluttering glance and then hurries off towards the 'offstage' 'stage right'.*)
MAGGIE	Managed to get your five and nine on then?
JAKE	(*inspecting himself in the stage-side mirror*) Sorry?
MAGGIE	Your slap. Your make-up.
JAKE	Yeah, well, I've a personal stylist.
MAGGIE	Nevertheless, ongoing, Mr Caffrey, you might # find it easier
JAKE	Jake.
MAGGIE	to be backstage by the half.
JAKE	The half?
	(*Unnoticed,* BERNIE BIGELOW *enters, dressed as* CAPTAIN BARNACLE; *his almost permanent companion* PISTACHIO, *dressed as* SEAMAN CUMMINGS, *is on his arm.* PISTACHIO *is a puppet monkey.* BERNIE *sits down, waiting patiently.*)
MAGGIE	I know that you're the headliner, lead singer with Blow or # whatever you're
JAKE	Breeze.
MAGGIE	called, our eponymous hero, etcetera, etcetera, but that's onstage. Out there, you are king. I don't argue with that, Mr Caffrey. But # back
JAKE	Jake.

MAGGIE   here, I rule. And there do need to be rules, for everyone's # sake . . .

JAKE   You're queen.

MAGGIE   You're quick.

JAKE   I don't want to lose my head.

MAGGIE   Well, be warned, I'll bite it off if you continue to encourage that mob of screaming # minxes.

BERNIE   (*to no one in particular*) St Genesius, the patron saint of actors, ended up decapitated.

MAGGIE   (*not heeding* BERNIE) They're making Fred at the stage door's life a misery. I realise that you need to schmooze with your coachloads, Mr Caffrey, but # please save

JAKE   Jake.

MAGGIE   it for later . . . Jake. Once the half is called, the only thing you should think about getting up is the curtain. Besides, can you really trust the sincerity of someone who hyperventilates before you've performed? So, you scratch my back, Jake, I'll let the stage door Julies do the same to yours. After curtain down. OK?

JAKE   (*kissing her*) OK. Wish me luck!

MAGGIE   It's bad luck to wish good luck in the theatre.

BERNIE   I always say "break an arm".

JAKE   (*like* MAGGIE, *ignoring* BERNIE) Who said?

MAGGIE   It's tradition.

JAKE   Well, you're the queen, change it. (*Beat.*) For me, please. I'm cacking myself. I've never done anything like this before.

MAGGIE   What? All those concerts at Wembley and # wherever and . . . (*Drying up.*) wherever else . . .

JAKE   I wasn't dressed like a medieval nonce, I didn't
                have to be funny, I didn't have to act. (*Beat.*)
                Wish me luck.

MAGGIE   Good luck. And if you're not in your dressing
                room by 6.55 tomorrow, you'll need it.

JAKE   (*heading off towards the stage*) Actually I was
                thinking of 1.55 tomorrow. Unless you don't
                need me at the matinée, ma'am.

                (JAKE *has gone.*)

BERNIE   You can see why all the girls take to him.

MAGGIE   I'm trying to maintain my legendary myopia.
                (*Beat.*) I haven't called you, Mr Bigelow.
                (*Consulting her script.*) You're not on for at
                least another twenty minutes.

BERNIE   Oh, no problems, Maggie. # I prefer it up here.

MAGGIE   (*realising*) Oh, I'm sorry. I sent Mr May to
                his room. He didn't really carry on exerting, #
                did he?

BERNIE   (*smiling broadly*) I really do. The roar of the
                greasepaint, the smell of the crowd. After all,
                each to his own. Live and let psyche-up, #
                that's what I say.

MAGGIE   Well, if you're happy just to sit there. Quietly.

BERNIE   Oh, Pistachio always gets tongue-tied before a
                first night. (*To* PISTACHIO.) Don't you?
                (PISTACHIO *nods energetically;* BERNIE *laughs
                good-naturedly.*)

MAGGIE   (*laughing*) Yes . . . (*Suddenly realising.*) Oh,
                shit, Wendy! (*Dashing to the tannoy.*)
                Wendy! Wendy! Miss Westcott-Hall! Sorry,
                pet, I forgot. You're supposed to be on! Don't
                bother about the tins, Jake can . . .

                (*She is interrupted by* WENDY, *now wearing
                full cat costume, dashing across, past* BERNIE

*and her, and onto stage, about half a dozen
tin cans tied to her tail and clattering
furiously.)*

(once WENDY *has gone, to the air)* . . . can
always improvise. (*Beat, during which* BERNIE
chuckles happily.) Fucking Keith.

BERNIE   (*smiling cheerily*) Ah, Maggie, nothing like a
first night!

MAGGIE   True, Bernie. More like something approaching
Bedlam.

BERNIE   Sorry?

MAGGIE   No, I have to confess I rather enjoy it. (*Into
tannoy.*) Tom, have you got the Sultan of
Morocco back from 'The Jolly Brewers'? He's
on in the dream sequence in five minutes.

                (*Blackout.*)

                (*When the lights snap back up, we are
                frontstage again, in London Town.*)

DICK   (*entering, with the traditional cloth bundle
                tied to a stick*) London at last! (*We assume
                that there's a fair amount of cheering;* DICK
                waits for it to die down.) How big it seems
                compared with the village of my birth. At this
                very moment, I'm beginning to wish I'd never
                left Pauntley. (*It should be noted that 'At This
                Very Moment' is obviously the name of* JAKE
                CAFFREY'S *latest hit. To audience.*) That's in
                Gloucestershire, for those too mean to buy a
                programme and read the very educational
                footnotes! Anyone would think you were just
                here to have fun! (*Obviously there are cheers
                from out front.*) What a fool I was though to
                believe the stories everyone told me. The
                streets of London were supposed to be paved
                with gold! Mud more like. And the people! So
                many, and not a kindly word for a poor

penniless boy without a friend in the whole city. Still, I'm just in time to see the Lord Mayor's show. One day I hope to be Lord Mayor myself, but it's going to be difficult without anyone to help me. You know, I thought this would be a breeze (*Loud cheering.*), but instead it's worse than a blur. This isn't an oasis; I'm a boy alone . . .

(*There is a loud mewing, off.*)

What's that?

(TOMMY THE CAT *hurries on, a length of string tied to his tail, to which have been attached several empty tin cans.* TOMMY *runs around trying to lose the cans, mewing plaintively.*)

Oh, the poor thing. I've got to help him. (*To* TOMMY.) Here, puss, here, puss!

(TOMMY *backs off, nervously.*)

It's all right. I'm not going to hurt you.

(TOMMY *comes in slightly.*)

There now . . . (*He approaches* TOMMY, *who backs off again, very concerned by the cans.*)

Poor creature, you're terribly nervous, aren't you? Anyone would think there were reviewers in tonight. I could help you with those cans if you like.

(TOMMY *is still suspicious.*)

If you'd trust me . . .

(*Both are still, then* TOMMY *approaches cautiously, sniffing at* DICK'S *hands.* DICK *is very careful not to scare him.* TOMMY *allows* DICK *to untie the cans.*)

There! That's better! (*As* TOMMY *twists about, enjoying freedom.*) Who did this to you? How

could they be so cruel? Did they come from
Canary Wharf?

(TOMMY *rubs himself against* DICK, *purring
loudly.*)

Oh, you don't need to thank me, Mr Cat. I'm
only too pleased to be able to help someone.
You're the first friendly face I've seen since I
arrived in London Town.

(TOMMY *meows, indicating himself.*)

You mean that you've only just arrived here
yourself?

(TOMMY *nods.*)

So, we're both strangers to the big City. Well,
in that case, let me introduce myself. (*Bowing.*)
I'm Richard Whittington, though most people
call me Dick. And what might your name be, I
wonder, Mr Tom Cat . . . ?

(TOMMY *nods.*)

Noddy?

(TOMMY *shakes his head.*)

Shaky?

(TOMMY *spells out the letters of his name with
his arms.*)

(*to audience*) Did he say "Tommy"?

(*Audience: Yes!*)

Are you sure?

(*Audience: Yes!!!*)

Well, of course! Mr Thomas Cat! Tom Cat!
Tommy to his friends!

(TOMMY *rubs up against him, and points to
him, meaningfully.*)

And I'm one of your friends? Well, I'm very glad, Tommy. Pleased to make your acquaintance. I must say that you're a very clever cat! And I'm going to need somebody clever around, if I'm ever to win my fortune.

(TOMMY *shows approval.*)

But I'm being forward. You must already have an owner . . .

(TOMMY *nods and points at* DICK.)

What? You mean me?

(TOMMY *nods decisively.*)

Well, I'd like to be your master and if you'd really want to stay with me, I'll be very pleased to . . .

(TOMMY *impulsively shakes his hand/paw.*)

Well, looks like we've got each other a partner, partner! Pussy and Dick. What an ideal combination!

(*And with that,* DICK *bursts into an up-tempo melody that no doubt suggests a recent 'Breeze' hit that featured* JAKE CAFFREY *on lead vocals. After a verse and chorus, or even less, during which* TOMMY *perhaps performs a form of soft-shoe shuffle, the lights snap out.*)

(*As the lights fade up, we are backstage once more.* NORMA *and* ROBIN *are sitting in the wings. She is smoking, as she always seems to be; he is trying to do the crossword, ditto.*)

NORMA   (*to* ROBIN) I know they seem quiet, but it's really that they're just concentrating, bless them. They're a *listening* audience. A very good first # night audience.

ROBIN   Listening, love? When I'm busting
             haemorrhoids trying to be funny, I want 'em to
             laugh, Norma, # not listen.

NORMA   It is marvellous to be back doing live theatre. I
             have missed it. Dearly. And it's so wonderful
             to get one's teeth into something # different. I
             mean, I love

ROBIN   Gnashers, eh?

NORMA   June Gladwell to death, # bless her,

ROBIN   You are getting into character, old love.

NORMA   don't get me wrong, but, well, thirteen years!
             One needs a rest, *she* needs a rest, # and it's
             lovely

ROBIN   We all do, love.

NORMA   to be able to show the fans that one is capable
             of something more. I remember when I was first
             offered June, I said, "Only for six months, a
             year maximum, I don't want to get typecast".
             But how it flies! I know it's only soap but, as I
             said to my husband Gerry, one can't be
             snobbish about these things. Soap opera's the
             modern day Mummers' Plays, or even
             Commedia Dell' Arte, but with social
             awareness. And, you know, the standard's
             remarkably high. When June had her cancer
             scare a while back, Hilary Kingsley said in 'The
             Daily Mirror' that if I'd given that performance
             at the RSC, I'd have won an Olivier. Of course,
             # I *was* at

ROBIN   (*who has drifted back to his crossword*)
             "Oddball Friar Tuck smashed right away on a
             drug". Um.

NORMA   the RSC. For many months. Yes, that episode
             attracted over eight million. Not 'EastEnders' I
             know, but very good for us. Actually, it was
             Hilary who called June the Lady Macbeth of

the WI. Very apt, I thought. Oh, yes, soap is
definitely the modern Shakespeare.

(*Beat.*)

ROBIN   (*finding the answer; triumphant*) Fruit cake!
               Of # course!

NORMA   (*looking at him sharply*) Sorry?

               (*The lights fade quickly on* ROBIN *and* NORMA.)

               (*. . . as they rise on* ANASTASIA *in her dressing
               room. She is applying her hairspray. A large,
               ostentatious bunch of flowers is in a vase on
               the table. She liberally sprays her hair, then
               squirts the flowers.* WENDY *enters.*)

ANASTASIA   Yes?

WENDY   Sorry to bother you, Miss Krabbe. (*She
               pronounces the last 'e', so it sounds like
               'crabby'.*) # But I . . .

ANASTASIA   (*correcting her sharply*) Krabbe. Come in.
               Entrez. About time. Service as shoddy as an
               Aeroflot steward. I have never met such a
               discourteous doorman, # and as for . . .

WENDY   (*edging in, clutching an elaborately wrapped
               bottle*) Sorry. I just # wanted to . . .

ANASTASIA   (*indicating her bathroom off*) It is through
               there. I would unblock it myself but I do not
               want to chip my nails.

               (WENDY *just stands there. Beat.*)

               Well? Shoo! # You

WENDY   I'm Wendy. Wendy playing Tommy. Wendy
               Westcott-Hall. We met at a few rehearsals.

ANASTASIA   are here to unblock the euphemism, are you
               not? (*Beat.*) Oh, yes, I do remember you.
               Vaguely. You are the . . . what is it called? SAS?

WENDY   ASM. Acting ASM actually. I act Tommy. I
             don't unblock # thingies . . .

ANASTASIA   Oh. Perhaps you should. (*Beat.*) Wendy
             Westcott-Hall. Sounds like a draughty
             ancestral home. They did not send you then?

WENDY   No, I came on my own.

ANASTASIA   Well, as you are here, # you

WENDY   Yes?

ANASTASIA   might as well have a go. (*She indicates off once
             more.*)

WENDY   (*holding up the wrapped bottle*) Actually, I
             came to give you this.

ANASTASIA   (*eyeing it suspiciously*) What is it?

WENDY   It's a first night present. For # good luck.

ANASTASIA   A present?

WENDY   From me to you. (*Then, in a fearful rush.*) To
             say how much I'm looking forward to working
             with you over the next five weeks and a bit,
             really thrilled, especially to be actually on
             stage together, even if it's only the one scene,
             though there's also the finalé of course, can't
             wait for that, I've seen tons of your films, on
             video of course, 'Tomorrow's Today's
             Yesterday', # that's Daddy's

ANASTASIA   'Today's Yesterday's Tomorrow'.

WENDY   all-time favourite, of all time . . . oh yes, and
             then the hospital ones, when you were the sexy
             nurse or patient or you-know and Leslie thingie
             was always chasing after you, # you were
             brilliant . . .

ANASTASIA   (*who has snatched the present and unwrapped
             it to find a bottle of whisky*) Silence! Shut up!
             Zip it! (WENDY *has stopped.*) Scotch?

WENDY   Yes.

ANASTASIA   Why?

WENDY   I thought you'd like it.

ANASTASIA   Why?

WENDY   Well, I was going to get flowers but when I
told Mummy that you were the Fairy of the
Bells, she said, "Oh, *that's* what she's on
nowadays", so I thought, oh, that's why
they've called the Fairy that, # like a
promotional gimmick or something, you
know . . .

ANASTASIA   Thank you. It is divine. Now, here is my
present, from me to # you. (*She holds up a
plunger with obvious distaste.*) You are

WENDY   But . . .

ANASTASIA   the acting AS. So act. ASAP.

WENDY   (*reluctantly taking the plunger*) But, Miss
Krabbé, # I'm not . . .

ANASTASIA   (*screaming*) Krabbe. The 'e' # is silent. There
is no acute accent and it is

WENDY   Well, you're always known just as Anastasia,
so I never knew how to . . .

ANASTASIA   not Middle English. I am not Krabbé. I am just
plain unadulterated Krabbe!

WENDY   (*beat; a little shell-shocked*) Right. I'll take
your word for that.

          (*As the lights blackout on* ANASTASIA *and*
WENDY . . .)

          (. . . *they rise again on* NORMA *and* ROBIN *in the
wings.* MAGGIE *is in her usual position, in
prompt corner.*)

MAGGIE (*to* NORMA) Miss Bailey, if you could get into position, I'll give the box the green light for the green smoke.

NORMA (*getting up and moving swiftly to* MAGGIE'S *prompt corner*) Of course. Can I just have a peek, dear? (*Consulting the script, reading aloud.*) "Right, that's it! I'm now severely stroppy. My blood starts to boil when things get soppy." (*Almost a wail.*) Oh, God, no wonder I can't remember them. They make one's toes and tongue twist up like fusilli! (*Hurrying onto stage.*) They're the written equivalent of fingernails down a blackboard. (*She has gone.*)

ROBIN (*to* MAGGIE) That's the origin of the term 'winging it', you know. Dashing into the wings to check your next ruddy line. I remember # my West

MAGGIE (*absorbed with something else*) I know.

ROBIN End début. With Dad, funnily enough. Crappy little thriller called 'Murder in Mind'. By then, pater had spent so many years in rep, a new play each week, that every Sunday for eight months, the poor old bugger had to relearn it all over again! (*Laughing uproariously.*) They were troopers in # those days.

MAGGIE (*into tannoy*) Tom. Tom, are you back? (*Beat.*) Ratshit.

ROBIN (*almost to himself*) I mean, look at old Wilf. Eighty, if he's a day, and still going strong. When Dad was starting out in the 'legitimate' theatre, Wilfred Raymond was his absolute bloody hero. 'Course, Wilf wasn't really legit. Weaned at the tough old titty of music hall. (*Chuckling.*) Never thought I'd end up acting alongside him. Funny business. (*Beat.*) We're both Water Rats, you know.

(NICK *and* BERNIE *enter from the stage;* BERNIE, *as always, is accompanied by* PISTACHIO.)

NICK   (*as he enters; to* BERNIE) It's just not going to work. I did say this to Quentin during rehearsals. # Why

BERNIE   I know.

NICK   do I say it?

BERNIE   (*smiling politely*) Well, Nick, I suppose because it's funny.

NICK   Yeah, but . . . I mean, come on, Bernie. You say, "I think therefore I am", and I say, "Isn't that putting Descartes before the horse?".

BERNIE   (*heading off to the dressing rooms*) Well, as I say, it's funny, Nick. # Hello, Robin. Good house.

NICK   (*pursuing* BERNIE *off*) Yes, but Christ, Bernie! Idle Jack wouldn't know who Descartes was. (*Beat; as he disappears after* BERNIE, *a thought strikes.*) Unless . . . hey, hold on, maybe that's why he's always so tired, sitting up all night reading German philosophy. Yeah, that's good, a whole new light, a new dimension, yeah, # that's very good. (*He, and* BERNIE, *have gone.*)

MAGGIE   (*into tannoy*) Tom! Please be there. Please be here. (*Beat.*) Soon.

            (SUZANNE *enters from the dressing rooms, dressed as an incongruously sexy rat.*)

SUZANNE   Hiya.*

ROBIN   Hello there, love.

MAGGIE   * One minute, stage right, the London sewers, another bit of dancing. # Hello.

(NICK *re-enters from the dressing rooms, obviously in pursuit of* SUZANNE. *He stops when he realises that, of course,* ROBIN *and* MAGGIE *are still there.*)

SUZANNE   I know, thank you.

MAGGIE   No need to, # it's my job.

NICK   Hi there.

            (*An embarrassed pause.*)

ROBIN   Hello there, love. (*Beat; looks at crossword.*) "Mixed-up dog's got no direction; no point hanging around for".

NICK   (*sharply*) Pardon?

ROBIN   (*innocently*) Four down.

NICK   (*to* SUZANNE) Don't forget, Suze, if it feels right, use it. It's your body, after all. Just remember, # you are

MAGGIE   (*into tannoy*) Tom!

NICK   not one of the chorus, Suzy. You are an individual surrounded by other individuals.

MAGGIE   All singing the same lines, wearing the same costumes # and dancing the same steps.

SUZANNE   Cheers, Nick, I'll remember that. Wish I'd had a proper drama school training. I'd be doing high-class classical stuff like you.

            (*She exits onto stage. Beat.*)

NICK   (*to* ROBIN *and* MAGGIE, *generally*) Just helping Suzy with her inner life . . . yeah . . . (*He tails off and then returns to the dressing rooms.*)

ROBIN   Yes, never thought I'd end up billed over Wilfred Raymond. Sad really. Still, does get his name in a box under the title: "And Wilfred Raymond as the Sultan of Morocco". Fifty years ago, he'd have had more fans out there than young whatisname. 'Course, now they'd all be underground or behind zimmers.

MAGGIE   Or helping Wilfred prop up the bar of 'The Jolly Brewers'. You know, they had to amend the original script to give him more pub time. First act: a three minute dream sequence. Just sits in a throne and gets fanned. No lines. No *reason* other than to prove he's actually in the show. Then no further appearance till the second half, # when he

ROBIN   The Hamlet wait.

MAGGIE   gets hoisted back on the throne, fanned again, says the very odd line, written large on the back of the fan, then time for a top-up before the walkdown. He certainly deserves some kind of box.

             (*Suddenly*, TOM NANCARROW *enters. He is wearing a tatty old raincoat, and a hat pulled down over his face.*)

MAGGIE   Tom! Thank Christ! You've got about two minutes.

TOM   I know, Mags, # I know.

             (*Frantically, he begins to unbutton and remove his raincoat,* MAGGIE *helping him.*)

MAGGIE   Did you get him?*

ROBIN   Wilfred?

TOM   * Yes, he was lecturing a hatstand on why Arthur Askey should never have been given an OBE.

MAGGIE   Did you get him back to his dressing room?

TOM   Yes, but I've locked the door, so please don't forget to let him out when the dream comes. I'd do it, but I'll just be coming off.

MAGGIE   I'll escort him to the throne personally, # don't
            worry.

TOM   Everything else going OK?

MAGGIE   Yes. For a first night. Still can't find Keith,
            Wendy's so nervous she'll get fur balls if
            she's not careful, and Norma's smoked so
            many Consulates she smells like a Polo mint
            factory. Oh, and Nick's dalliance with that
            dancer, that none of us are supposed to know
            about, looks like it's coming to an end.

TOM   Good. Only another five and a half weeks and
            sixty performances to go. (*By now he has got
            out of his raincoat to reveal a colourful dame
            costume.* TOM *is playing* SARAH THE COOK.)
            Right, ask the band to give me an extra sixteen
            bars to get my rug on. (*As he hurries off.*) God
            help us, everyone.

MAGGIE   (*into tannoy*) Pete, can you play Sarah's intro
            twice over, old cock?

            (*Beat.*)

ROBIN   Bernie was telling me about this old girl when
            he started off at Pontins, Great Yarmouth.
            Spent the summers soft-shoe shuffling at the
            end of Britannia Pier, then come winter,
            insisted on turning up at the camp and doing
            likewise as Mother Goose. Anyway, one night,
            middle of a routine, the poor old dear tripped
            over her own flippers, and fell slap bang onto
            her beak. Broke her nose. Bernie and Co got
            her up but she just carried on. Well, her front,
            all white feathers, started to go crimson with
            blood, but, great old trooper, she just carried
            on till the end of the scene. Apparently, in the
            paint and crayons class next day, all the kids
            drew this tap-dancing red robin.

            (*Beat.*)

MAGGIE   Well, I suppose it was Christmas. (*Beat.*) It's Godot, by the way. (*Beat;* ROBIN *looks at her, bemused.*) Four down.

(*Blackout.*)

(*Lights up on the forestage, outside Fitzwarren's Stores.*)

SARAH   (*entering, with a shopping bag in each hand, and seeing the audience*) Who said "Who's the bag in the middle?" Hello, my little petit-fours. I'm Sarah. Sarah the cook, the Alderman's cook who cooks for Alderman Fitzwarren. I rule the roast around here. Oh, what a lovely man my little itsy-bitsy Fitzy is! Try saying that without your own teeth. It's strange, girls, but he looks just like my fourth husband. Not that he knows that yet. You see, I've only had three so far. Well, you're allowed sixteen, aren't you? It says so: four better, four worse, four richer, four poorer. I met my first husband under unfortunate circumstances: we were single. I shall never forget our first kiss: hot and sizzling. He forgot to take the fag out of his mouth. Oh, but our courtship! Fast and furious. I was fast; he was furious. I would say it was also rough and ready, but it's pretty much the same punchline. (*Explaining the gag to an audience member.*) Rough, ready . . . (*To the rest of the audience.*) The gates are down, the lights are flashing, but the train's not coming. But anyway I'll go back to my first husband. That'll upset him. My second husband I met just after the war. Oh, he had a marvellous war record. Vera Lynn singing 'We'll Meet Again'. Unfortunately for us, we did. No, but seriously, he fought with 'em all: Wavell in Tobruk, Mountbatten in Burma and Monty at the Bulge. He couldn't get on with anyone! You know, he was in France when they fired the very first shot. Australia when they fired the second. So then I got engaged to a contortionist. Till he broke

it off. Finally, I married an all-in wrestler. I
remember thinking, "If it's all in, why wrestle?"
Save yourselves, it's a very weak finish . . . So
anyway now I'm young, free and single. Well,
two out of three ain't bad. And just waiting for
Fitzy to pop the question. I'll have him eating
out of the palm of my hand. Well, it saves on
the washing-up, doesn't it? Imagine it! Sarah
Fitzwarren! (*Picking on one man in
particular.*) Oh, and look, there's Warren!
(*Taking a banana out of her bag and throwing
it at him.*) There, you go, luv, a reject, but I
didn't think you'd mind a bent one.

(*Blackout.*)

Friday 17th December – second night

The lights fade up to reveal BERNIE, *sitting patiently in the
wings with* PISTACHIO, *and* SALLY, *intermittently chomping on
an apple and mid-conversation with* MAGGIE *in prompt corner.*

SALLY   (*to* MAGGIE) I just don't want to be
                 stereotyped: Sally Musto. TV weathergirl.
                 Sponsored by Powertex. (*Beat.*) I'm an
                 intelligent person, Maggie. A published
                 meteorologist. I was at Cambridge. I don't
                 want to be labelled as a TV bimbo. I won't be.
                 # I've a first-rate brain.

MAGGIE   So you decide to play the dippy heroine in a
                 number two tour panto? Um. This trip to
                 Cambridge, pet, was it a day's punting or did
                 you splash out on a long weekend? (*Into
                 tannoy.*) Robin. One minute or it's the
                 paedophile exclusive in the local 'Chronicle'.

                 (*Before* SALLY *can muster a reply,* NICK *enters
                 from the dressing rooms, ready for his entrance.*)

NICK   Sal! How's it going? The vibes feeling good #
                 tonight?

SALLY   Oh, not so bad. Except for Robin.

NICK   Robin? What's he done now? *

MAGGIE   Keeps being Robin.

SALLY   * Keeps ad libbing. It's only the second night
               and he's bored already. For instance, in our
               first 'town square' scene, he has to say,
               "Which one?" and I say, "The one on the left,
               Father". And he said, totally different to the
               script, "Stage left, or from where they're
               looking?" Meaning the audience. Of course,
               they all collapsed laughing, whilst I was left
               floundering, # desperately trying to stick to the
               text.

               (MAGGIE *chuckles, as does* BERNIE, *quietly.*)

NICK   (*outraged*) That's just outrageous, not on at
               all. Mind you, Sal, what can you expect? It
               sums him up. Panto, thrillers, French farces.
               That's not real theatre, Sal. # And Robin's not

MAGGIE   It is as far as this town's concerned.

NICK   a real actor. # I mean I'm all for

SALLY   Don't get me wrong, I like Robin very much,
               it's only . . .

NICK   living on the edge, being 110 percent in the
               moment, letting the impulse take you, but
               that's unforgivable. That kind of cheap gag
               destroys the suspension of disbelief, tears
               down the fourth wall in completely the wrong
               way . . . I mean, I'm all for crossing the divide,
               challenging the audience, subverting the
               traditional concepts, but that # kind of
               cretinous . . .

MAGGIE   (*over-riding him, as* BERNIE *gets up to leave*)
               Remind me, Mr May, when exactly did you
               graduate from 'the Academy'?

NICK   A year ago last Autumn. Why?

MAGGIE   And this is your first professional
          engagement?

NICK   Well . . . I did that telly ad for Whiskas and
          two voiceovers for Mr Clutch . . . (*He dries up;
          a phenomenon.*)

MAGGIE   As I say. (*Beat.*) All that free time, you really
          should consider hiring a hall and holding
          masterclasses. As it is, it's all such a waste.
          (*Before* NICK *can answer, to* BERNIE, *who's
          sidling off.*) We boring you, Bernard?

BERNIE   (*pleasantly*) No, no, just going to stretch my
          legs.

PISTACHIO And his arms.

          (*Both* BERNIE *and* MAGGIE *laugh.*)

NICK   (*to* SALLY) Look, I told you, you can see his
          lips moving like a nutter on the bus.

BERNIE   (*to* NICK, *politely*) Sorry? *

NICK   Nothing.

MAGGIE   * (*quietly*) I hear you got a fan letter today,
          Bernie.

BERNIE   Yes. Quite a surprise. Pleasant, # of course.

MAGGIE   That'll be your fifth # already, won't it? *

NICK   (*to* SALLY) Jake gets over fifty a day.

BERNIE   * Eh, fourth.

MAGGIE   (*to* NICK) You been giving our local postie a
          hernia, Mr May?

NICK   I don't pursue art for adulation.

MAGGIE   Well, that's a stroke of luck, isn't it? (*Without
          pause.*) By the way, old cock, you just missed
          your cue.

(*A horrified beat, then* NICK *rushes off, onto the stage.*)

(*to his retreating figure*) Just remember: focus!

SALLY   (*to* BERNIE) Who was it from, Bernie? The letter. I only get rather worrying ones asking me to dinner.

BERNIE   A long-time fan, apparently, Sally. Apparently followed me and old Pistachio since we did 'Pistachio's Nutty Newstime' for the Beeb.

PISTACHIO   Less of the old!

(SALLY *and* BERNIE *laugh, as* WENDY *enters from the dressing rooms and goes to* MAGGIE *in prompt corner.*)

SALLY   I used to watch that when I was young. I loved it. I wish I was old enough to have seen 'Nuts to School!' My elder sister used to tell us all about it. She absolutely . . . (*She stops.*) Oh, I'm sorry.

BERNIE   No, no, totally all right. It was quite a while back.

PISTACHIO   Even the cameramen had to wear DJs.

(BERNIE *laughs and exits towards the dressing rooms;* SALLY *is left behind, not laughing quite so much.*)

WENDY   Hello, Maggie. Private WWH reporting # for duty.

MAGGIE   Where've you been?

WENDY   I popped in to see Miss (*Carefully.*) Krabbe. To apologise for last night. # The flood . . .

MAGGIE   It wasn't your fault, pet. She should have waited for # maintenance.

WENDY   Have you seen Nick?

MAGGIE   Yes, but thankfully the moment passed.

SALLY   He's just gone on stage.

WENDY   (*obviously disappointed*) Oh, right.

MAGGIE   More to the point, have you seen Keith?

WENDY   No.

MAGGIE   Ditto.

             (SALLY *sits down and begins to eat a banana
             or something equally healthy.*)

             So here I am, lumbered. My only help an ASM
             with more stage time than Hamlet. How did you
             manage to get around the unions? ASMs don't
             act # anymore.

WENDY   Dad. He's on the board of KTMP.

MAGGIE   Ah! Our beloved sponsors. I suppose if
             Daddy was Chairman, you'd be playing her
             (*Indicating* SALLY.) part.

WENDY   Oh, no. He says I need to start at the bottom
             and work my way up.

MAGGIE   Thank God for our modern meritocracy.

WENDY   (*secretively, to* MAGGIE) Last night, Daddy
             was telling me all about Mr Nancarrow and (*her
             voice dropping*) his boyfriend.

             (WENDY'S *voice not dropping that low,* SALLY
             begins to listen in.)

MAGGIE   Oh, yes?

WENDY   He said that Mr Nancarrow's . . . friend started
             off running this place # and then . . .

MAGGIE   Barry Nelson. Yes, for over twenty years.

WENDY   Then he started . . . seeing Tom, # Mr
             Nancarrow,

MAGGIE	(*monotone*) Seeing, acting with, screwing, living with . . .
WENDY	and they began to run # it together.
MAGGIE	Yes, run it together. Daddy's spot on so far. Does he take the board minutes?
WENDY	No, I don't think so. (*Beat.*) He's right then?
MAGGIE	Oh, yes. Tom and Barry ran "this place" for nearly fourteen years. They were quite a double act. Off stage and on. (*Beat.*) Nelson & Nancarrow. Played the Ugly Sisters year on year, without a break, for thirteen seasons. Loveliest Uglies I ever saw.
SALLY	So where's Barry now?
MAGGIE	(*very matter-of-fact*) Oh, he died. Six months ago. (*Beat.*) That's why we're not doing 'Cinderella'.

(*The lights snap out . . .*)

(. . . *then snap up to reveal* FITZWARREN *and* SARAH, *in front of the Stores.*)

FITZWARREN	Where is that lazy son of yours, Sarah? Late for work again! Only me and Alice to mind the store. If you weren't his mother, I'd sack him.
SARAH	You can't sack Jack. He does the work of four people.
FITZWARREN	Well, show me the other three and I'll sack them too.
SARAH	Those three. (*To audience.*) Innumerate and illiterate. See, I told you he needed looking after.
FITZWARREN	I'm not the ignoramus. Your son, Idle Jack, is. A gross ignoramus.
SARAH	144 times worse than an ordinary ignoramus? Oh, no, Fitzy, he's smarter than he looks.

FITZWARREN	He'd need to be. Take it from a businessman, when his IQ reaches fifty, he should sell.
SARAH	Ah, now, selling, yes! The customers love him. When he's here. But then he's always been very courteous to his inferiors.
FITZWARREN	Beats me where he finds them!
SARAH	Oh, Fitzy, it takes all sorts of people to make up the world.
FITZWARREN	Too bad he's not one of them.
SARAH	I don't have to stand here and be dressed down by you. I can go in the kitchen and let Warren do it. (*As she goes, to 'Warren' in the audience.*) Just give me five minutes, Warren, then pop in with your banana and we can knock up something fruity. (*To* FITZWARREN.) See, a real man! He can't wait to see me turnover steaming on the table. (*To audience.*) Au revoir, my little vol-au-vents! (*She exits.*)
FITZWARREN	Oh dear, kids, I've upset Sarah. I don't want to lose her. She's an excellent cook. You know, she can cut four loaves of bread at the same time. I call her my lucky four-loaf cleaver. Still she's an even better magician. She can turn anything into an argument. She just goes on without knowing when to get off. And here comes the cause of it all! Idle Jack!
	(IDLE JACK *enters, with a 'Do not disturb' sign around his neck, and carrying an alarm clock and teddy.*)
	Ah, there you are! And how d'you find yourself this morning?
JACK	Well, I just pulled back the covers and there I was. Mind you, yesterday morning, I woke up

to find I was under the bed. I must be a little potty.

FITZWARREN   You are! This is the third time this week you've been late for work. Don't you have an alarm clock at home?

JACK   'Course we do, but there's nine of us in the family and Mum only sets it for eight.

FITZWARREN   You should have been here an hour ago!

JACK   Why? What happened?

FITZWARREN   Where have you been?

JACK   Having my hair cut.

FITZWARREN   In the firm's time?

JACK   Well, it grows in the firm's time.

FITZWARREN   It doesn't all grow in the firm's time.

JACK   I didn't have it all cut off.

FITZWARREN   Do you know what time you start work?

JACK   Yes, about half an hour after I get here.

FITZWARREN   I've a good mind to hire another assistant this very minute.

JACK   Oh, I wish you would. We'd get a lot more done if there were two of us.

FITZWARREN   (*to audience*) Somewhere a village is being deprived of an idiot. (*To* JACK.) You are the laziest person I've ever employed and as soon as I can find someone trustworthy, I'm replacing you.

JACK   Oh, no, please don't. I know I've got low standards . . .

FITZWARREN   Yes, and you still fail to achieve them. Even when you do turn up, you're next to useless.

JACK   Oh, don't put yourself down!

FITZWARREN   Why is it every time I walk into the store, I
                catch you standing there doing nothing?

JACK   Perhaps it's because you've rubber soles on
                and I can't hear you coming.

FITZWARREN   Well, you'll soon be going. (*To audience, as he
                begins to exit.*) Honestly! That boy's reached
                rock bottom, and started to dig.

                (*Blackout.*)

Sunday 19th December

The lights reveal JAKE *waiting in the wings.* SUZANNE, *now in
pixie costume, is very close.* MAGGIE *and* WENDY *are further
off, in prompt corner.*

SUZANNE   (*quietly, to* JAKE) So what about later then?

JAKE   (*even quieter*) Yeah, maybe, got a few friends
                in though. Might go for a curry # later or
                something.

SUZANNE   I could wait in your hotel room. The doorman
                knows me now almost as well as you. # Don't
                worry about waking me.

JAKE   Yeah, but I might not make it back.

SUZANNE   Fine. I'll get a good night's kip. The Grand
                sure beats the dump I'm in.

MAGGIE   (*interrupting loudly*) You two ready to
                perform then?*

JAKE   As I'll ever be.

SUZANNE   * Yeah. Cheers.

WENDY   Oh, you're doing awfully well, Jake. They
                adore you. Don't they, Suzanne? # (*Back to*
                JAKE.) You

SUZANNE	Yeah.
WENDY	know it.
JAKE	Yeah, well, # maybe . . .
WENDY	How many lust letters today?
JAKE	About sixty. # Thereabouts.
WENDY	That's more than everyone else put together.
MAGGIE	In their entire lives. OK, Jake, you're on. Break something flaccid.
SUZANNE	(*as she leaves*) That'd be hard.
MAGGIE	Then that'd be a contradiction.

(NICK *appears from the stage.*)

NICK	(*grabbing him earnestly*) Oh, Jake, mate, glad I caught you. You're blazing out there tonight, fucking blazing. # You are one talented fucker, just need
JAKE	Oh, well thanks, Nick, appreciate it.
NICK	a bit of technique, a bit of # training, and then . . .
MAGGIE	Excuse me, but the elves and pixies seem to have mislain Dick. They're now wandering aimlessly around like Japanese tourists who've lost their cameras.
JAKE	Sorry, Maggie, my queen. # Nick, gotta go, catch you later. (*He dashes off stagewards.*)
NICK	Oh, right. Just remember, Jake, it's your body, mate. (*To the others.*) Some professional tuning, and he'll go far.
MAGGIE	Beats me he got where he is today without you.
NICK	(*apparently not having heard*) I mean, at a really, *really* basic level, I bet he's never even questioned what motivates him.

MAGGIE   The sensible money's got to be on the
              gorgeous, gagging-for-it groupies and the even
              tastier sponsorship. Call me # a purist, but . . .

WENDY   Maggie! Please! (*Beat;* MAGGIE *withdraws to
              prompt corner.*) Nick, I was wondering if you
              were free tonight, after we fin . . . (*Correcting
              herself.*) I mean, *post-show.* Because I could
              really do with talking about why Tommy warms
              so quickly to Dick, and then follows # him to
              London, where obviously he's been treated
              really . . . (*She fizzles out.*)

NICK   Ah, sorry, Wend! I really need to get back to
              my digs, do some more research. Still haven't
              got to the bottom of this feller Jack. Though
              I've an instinct that Nietzsche might well hold
              the key.

WENDY   Oh, right, well, # no sweat, eh?

NICK   Another evening, yeah? # Tell you what I always

WENDY   Yeah, tomorrow . . . or whenever. Five more
              weeks after all.

NICK   find useful, is just sitting on your own,
              contemplating the character. (*As he edges
              away.*) Maybe start with thinking: if Tommy
              were an animal, what kind of animal would he be?

              (*Beat.*)

WENDY   Right.

              (NICK *begins some rather urgent breathing
              exercises, which involve a fair bit of puffing
              and grimacing.*)

MAGGIE   Wendy. Could you go and check on Wilfred.
              Oh, and apparently Anastasia wants a word. #
              (*As* WENDY *moves off.*) But remember,
              sweetheart, you are not her

WENDY   (*moving off*) Oh, fine, sure.

MAGGIE   PA or dresser. You've enough to do helping run the show and wagging your tail, so don't stand for any of her errand-running crap.

WENDY   Oh, I don't mind, Maggie. She talks about Hollywood.

MAGGIE   Pet, she's already been talking to you about it longer than she was there. Two films, and three husbands. Besides her own. That was it. After that, it was art-house all the way down. So, be pleasant, but no need for more. # She isn't

WENDY   But, Maggie . . .

MAGGIE   any different to all the rest. Just lives her hype a lot better. (*Beat.*) I need a fag.

WENDY   (*exiting, smiling, past* NICK) Okey dokey.

MAGGIE   (*to* NICK) Things could be worse, Mr May. You could be here in person. (*Into the tannoy.*) Miss Bailey to # the stage, please.

NICK   What?

MAGGIE   (*smiling sweetly*) Instead of one hundred percent in character.

           (*Just then,* SALLY *enters, heading for the stage.* NICK *immediately terminates exercising and approaches her.*)

NICK   Sal! Well met. What did you think of that first scene? # All over the fucking place or what? This eve', shelve

SALLY   Well, not bad, I suppose.

NICK   any plans. We need to work. I insist.

SALLY   That's very sweet, Nick, but # I really would rather have an early night.

NICK   No 'but's, Sal. It needs work. Forget the
             audiences and the crits; think about yourself.*

SALLY   Yes, well . . .

MAGGIE   * Quite right, Mr May. Think about yourself. I
             make it three minutes and counting before
             you're on. In night-cap and gown.

NICK   (*meaningfully to* SALLY) We'll talk, OK?

SALLY   OK.

             (NICK *hurries off to his dressing room.*)

MAGGIE   (*to* SALLY) Did you get the message that your
             mum called?

SALLY   No, # when?

MAGGIE   Between the shows. Fred took it. Tried you on
             the mobile but it was switched off.

SALLY   Stolen actually. # I did tell her.

MAGGIE   Well, use the payphone.

SALLY   She's not too happy me being up here. # Well,
             we've

MAGGIE   Oh, yes?

SALLY   always been a very close family, and it's
             Christmas, and so . . . (*She stops.*)

MAGGIE   It's a time for families.

SALLY   Yes. She knows I'll be back Christmas Day and
             for New Year, but . . .

MAGGIE   I can't comment, pet. I live here.

SALLY   I know what she means. It's not like Christmas.
             I'm used to being with the people I'm close to.
             I suppose it might be better here if we all lived
             together, # but we're so scattered. Different
             digs, B&Bs, hotels . . . no wonder

MAGGIE   Not too sure of that, petal.

SALLY   actors love playing Rattigan. 'Separate Tables'.
                We went to see it as a family treat. Meant
                nothing at the time.

MAGGIE   I could tell you're a scientist. Hit the nail.
                Separate tables, separate lives. Ignore Tom.
                For all the camaraderie bollocks, it's a very
                lonely profession. If I were you, angel, I'd
                stick to the weather. Michael Fish or no
                Michael Fish, it's far more predictable.

                (*Quick fade.*)

                (*A spotlight discovers* NORMA *on the payphone
                to her husband, a menthol cigarette
                permanently in, or to, hand.*)

NORMA   Oh, it's absolutely ghastly, Gerry. They keep
                hissing at me, every time they see me, every
                time I so much as open my mouth, they hiss.
                And boo. (*Beat.*) I am talking about the
                audience, darling, do kёep up. (*Beat.*) I know
                I'm Queen Rat, darling, I could hardly forget it,
                I'm sitting here looking like an imploded after-
                dinner mint. But Max told me it was an honour
                . . . the strongest dramatic role in the piece.
                (*Pause.*) The Shakespeare? Oh, yes, they've
                "inserted" it. Very painfully. All the subtlety
                of a mugging. A bit of Lear, Tempest. I even
                get to bowdlerise, or more like bugger-up,
                Henry Five. They've chucked in The Scottish
                Play too. Double, double, toil and dipshit
                drivel. (*Beat.*) He told me this was "the ideal
                vehicle" to return to stage work. God, if I'd
                wanted to commit theatrical hara-kiri, I'd have
                joined 'The Mousetrap', not the Rat Trap . . .
                How are the girls? You are making sure
                Annabel's eating properly, aren't you, Gerry?
                (*Beat.*) Well, done, darling. Remind her she
                won't get into the Royal Ballet on a diet of
                cottage cheese and Red Bull. (*Beat.*) I mean I
                should be Bowbells. What kind of perverse

casting is that? I'm the Londoner and they
give Fairy Bowbells to a woman who thinks
Canary Wharf's some kind of bird vomit.
(*Pause.*) I *am* a Londoner, darling! Well, I
once had those digs in Shepherds Bush. With
that shifty landlord I swore was Lord Lucan.
How did Lucy's swimming finals go, by the
way? (*Beat.*) Silver! Oh, bless her. Is she
there? (*Pause.*) Oh, well, give her my love. Tell
her I'll phone the same time tomorrow. And
gold next time! (*Pause.*) Well, I'll try in-
between the two shows then. I think Max has
lost interest. Provided he gets his ten per, he
couldn't care less. None of them realise I did
actually play Ariel. At the Royal Exchange.
Michael Billington found me "effective".
(*Beat.*) Of course it's in the biog, darling, but
they only buy the prog for the glossies and the
puzzles. They don't read it. Most of them
probably can't. (*Beat.*) But they keep hissing
at me, Gerry. I said to Max, I said, "Max, if I've
got to do panto, why not Cinderella? The title
role of". He just laughed. (*Beat.*) Yes, exactly
like that, Gerald. Just so. None of us are
getting any younger, but you needn't rub it in
like a Mongolian masseuse. (*Pause.*) So the
girls are missing me are they? (*Beat.*) Bless
them. You coping with the new dishwasher
OK? Good. And third bloody billing! Beneath
Cliff Richard and Mata Hari. Judi and Maggie
don't have to do this. If they can get out of it,
why oh why can't I? (*Beat.*) They're all miked,
you know, Gerry. Still, that's film and pop
videos for you: no training, no projection. I
mean Jake's a sweet boy but he'd never handle
the Olivier, like I have. Same with her,
Anastasia-no-surname-no-knickers. Less
famous for the few films she's made than the
many men she's laid. (*Beat; possibly close to
tears.*) Oh, Gerry, darling, help me, I've started
to rhyme.

(*Blackout.*)

(*The lights rise on* ALICE, DICK *and* TOMMY *outside Fitzwarren's Stores.*)

ALICE   Oh, how can I ever thank you, mysterious
          stranger? You and your cat have saved my life.
          Those evil, foul and generally despicable rats
          would have killed me.

DICK   Oh, my lady, it was nothing more than your
          average caring, sensitive and courageous boy
          and cat next door would do.

ALICE   You're wrong.

DICK   You're right. We don't live next door.

ALICE   Where do you live?

DICK   At this very moment, nowhere.

ALICE   Who are you? From whence do you come?
          Whither do you go? Wherefore? How? And why?

DICK   (*without pause*) Dick Whittington.
          Gloucestershire. To make my fortune. It's the
          key plot driver and my character's motivation.
          God only knows. Ditto.

ALICE   Oh, Dick, you've got all the answers!

DICK   Not to the most important question. The one,
          at this very moment, closest to my heart.

ALICE   Which is?

DICK   No, that's not it.

ALICE   Well, what is it?

DICK   That neither, but you're getting warmer.

ALICE   (*excited; her heart a-flutter*) Oh, Dick! Do ask
          it, ask it do!

DICK   Well, all right then. Nothing ventured, Tommy,
          nothing gained.

(TOMMY *crosses his fingers.*)

(*to* ALICE) Well, er . . . what's your name?

ALICE   Alice. Alice Fitzwarren. Was that the
             question?

DICK   No, I was just asking your name. And it is a
             beautiful one. (*To audience.*) She's so lovely,
             she takes my breath away. (*To* ALICE.) But a
             name no beautifuller than you deserve. (*To
             audience.*) And my grammar. (*To* ALICE.)
             Alice . . .

ALICE   Yes, Dick?

DICK   (*at once*) Do you know where I can find a job?

ALICE   (*disappointed*) A job? Oh.

             (TOMMY r*eacts; possibly hits his head, or even*
             DICK.)

DICK   I don't care what it is: boring choring, packing,
             stacking, humping, dumping. I'm not afraid of
             hard work. (*To audience.*) I've sung with
             Dannii Minogue after all.

ALICE   Well, my father, Alderman Fitzwarren, of
             Fitzwarren & Daughter, Purveyors of Prime,
             Premier and Pricey Produce, Provisions and
             Paraphernalia to Princes, Peers and Prosperous
             Parishioners, might have a vacancy.

             (TOMMY *points to himself.*)

DICK   Would he have two? Tommy and I are very
             close; we come as a pair. If you've a lot of
             jobs, you'll need a job lot.

ALICE   Well, he is cute.

DICK   And useful. He'll wipe out your rats at a swipe.

             (TOMMY *hands* ALICE *an oversized business
             card.*)

ALICE   (*Reading from the card*) "Mr Thomas Cat.
             Purring. Mating. Vermin hating.
             Exterminating". (*Beat.*) "Mouse calls
             welcome." (*Pause, whilst* DICK *and* TOMMY
             look at her expectantly.) Well, I'm sure we
             can persuade Father. Together. After all, less
             rats equal more customers.

DICK   And more work for me. Scores more stores
             chores! And then . . . fame and fortune!

ALICE   As the night follows day, and the moon the
             sun . . .

DICK   And then Alice . . .

ALICE   Yes, Dick?

             (*A significant moment.* DICK *then looks at*
             TOMMY *significantly.* TOMMY *slowly smooches
             off, whistling, eyes raised skywards, just as
             significantly.*)

DICK   Then, Alice, I'll be able to vouchsafe the
             question, at this very moment, verily dearest to
             my vibrating heart.

ALICE   Pop the query you really want to probe, Dick?

DICK   Oh, Alice, the forecast is sunshine after the
             rain, a cold front followed by a warm twister
             coming in from behind.

ALICE   Oh, Dick! Roll on tomorrow at 14.00 hours GMT!

             (*The happy couple possibly break into a song
             to the tune of the 'Sleeping Beauty Waltz' and
             dance a bit, before the lights lose them.*)

Tuesday 21st December

The lights rise backstage. ANASTASIA *is in mid-exit, speaking
to* TOM. MAGGIE *is in prompt corner, whilst* ROBIN *looks on,
the obligatory crossword on his lap.*

ANASTASIA	That waltz is ridiculous, Mr Nancarrow.
TOM	It's Tchaikovsky. # I thought you'd like it. Russian.
ANASTASIA	Precisely. It is the 'Sleeping Beauty Waltz'. It should be in 'Sleeping Beauty', not 'Dick Whittington'.
TOM	But there isn't a 'Dick Whittington Waltz'.
ANASTASIA	(*exiting*) Only because the bastard behind this horseshit was too lazy to fucking write one!

(*The grande dame has gone, dressing room-wards.*)

ROBIN	You ought to be careful, love. She used to be big, you know.
TOM	It was just the pantos that got small, yes, thank you, Robin.
MAGGIE	Robin, you're on. What are you waiting for?
ROBIN	My renaissance, love.

(*With a flourish,* ROBIN *exits to stage.*)

MAGGIE	(*to* TOM) If he's even five years older than me, I'll eat Norma's costume. Acts like my grandmother with a combined hangover and hernia. # I don't know how or why
TOM	Do grannies get hernias?
MAGGIE	you put up with all their crap . . .
TOM	Well, one of us has to resist the temptation to lob it back like a bile-coated cannonball.
MAGGIE	Robin's bearable, but that arse-talking Anastasia, the good time that's been had by all. She's as Russian as my Aunty Mabel.
TOM	This would be Aunt Mabel Mabelovnavich Kalabushnikov?

MAGGIE   The very same. (*Indicating off.*) Bethnal Green
           born and bred, I bet you. By the end of this
           run, they'll be more keys to her hotel room in
           circulation than on a concert grand piano.

TOM   Oh, Mags, that's rather harsh. A baby grand, #
           perhaps.

MAGGIE   She's already worked her way through the
           three straight boys in the chorus and we
           haven't been up a week. We've over a month
           to go yet and there's only eight in the band.

TOM   Wish I could lend a hand.

MAGGIE   By Week Four, that might be enough.

TOM   Mags, this isn't like you, # what's up?

MAGGIE   Oh, but it is.

           (*At this point*, NICK *and* BERNIE *appear from
           onstage, having just finished a scene.* NICK *is
           talking,* BERNIE *is accompanied by* PISTACHIO.)

NICK   I do think that's the way to deliver it, Bernie.
           Hope you don't mind me mentioning it.

BERNIE   Certainly not, Nick. Always open to
           suggestions. Handy hints. Top tips.
           Listening to someone with more experience.

NICK   Pleasure, Bernie. Like that 'portable' gag. I
           think there's real layers there. Loaded with
           pathos. "Captain, I've just made a portable."

BERNIE   And I say, "A portable what, Jack?"

NICK   "I don't know yet. I've only made the handle."
           (*Beat.*) Christ, Bernie, that one line gives so
           much away.

PISTACHIO (*unexpectedly*) Well, the way you're delivering
           it, you cunt, it certainly gives away any chance
           of a fucking laugh.

BERNIE   (*as he and* PISTACHIO *exit dressing room-*
                wards) Ha-ha, oh, dear me, sorry, Nick. Now
                Pistachio, shush.

NICK   No, Bernie, don't apologise for him. Let him
                speak. I think he's mined something crucial
                there. Maybe that's what Jack yearns for:
                approbation. Jeez, I never saw that before. (*As*
                he pursues them off.) Why does he make
                everything into a joke?

TOM   Exit, pursued by a bore.

MAGGIE   We've got problems there.

TOM   I know, Mags, I have to share a stage with them.

MAGGIE   They have to share a dressing room. *That's*
                the problem. I was wondering if we could try
                rejigging. Give Bernie a bit more space. You
                heard about his bankruptcy hearing.

TOM   Read about it. I don't think it's on, *The Stage*
                reporting that kind of thing. Especially after all
                the business Bernie's given them over the
                years. The money he's spent on Directory ads,
                by now he should own the ungrateful rag. #
                So, I'll see what I can do.

MAGGIE   Well, see what you can do.

                (*Beat.*)

                Still no sign of Keith. The company techie's
                gone, too. Some love match or other. Looks
                like a set up.

TOM   But only just. If they'd skipped off to Gretna
                Green a day earlier, the court of Morocco'd
                look like the Black Hole of Calcutta.

MAGGIE   Well, Wendy and I can cope.

TOM   How's she panning out?

MAGGIE   If enthusiasm were all. (*Beat.*) She's not the
            brightest kid. Been bungee-jumping with too
            long a rope.

            (*She sneezes.*)

TOM   Bless you.

MAGGIE   Save it for Wendy. She needs all the divine
            intervention she can get. In five years, she'll
            have given it all up to marry some rich, thick
            City type and spend her days lunching,
            shopping, interviewing nannies, and sweating
            it off at the Sanctuary.

TOM   Well, it's tough, but someone's got to do it.
            (*Mock-affectedly.*) One asks oneself: did one
            lose one's way?

MAGGIE   Poor cow nearly electrocuted herself yesterday
            matinée. We have got to sort out the wiring in
            The Old Girl, Tom. Only last # week

TOM   I know, Mags, I know. I'm getting to it.

MAGGIE   I got a shock, switched on the workers and the
            whole # bloody kit

TOM   Yes, all right, Mags, I know.

MAGGIE   and caboodle cut out. It's a bloody dump,
            Tom, and don't keep just saying "you know",
            Tom, because we both know . . .

            (*She is interrupted by* NORMA, *entering from
            the dressing rooms.*)

NORMA   Hello, Maggie dear, Tom darling, is Bernard off?

MAGGIE   Dressing room, Norma.

NORMA   No. There was just that boy there. Poor
            Bernard's taken to decamping to my room.
            Such a sensitive, darling man. A true
            gentleman, poet, fisherman, even shoots with
            gentry. A Lord's Taverner, no less. We have a

'cuppa', as June would say, and talk about real theatre. Or real variety in Bernard's case. I've just put on the Lapsang Souchong. # Perhaps our paths

TOM   Oh, nice.

NORMA   crossed in the labyrinth. (*Turning to go.*) He might be waiting for me.

TOM   Happy brewing!

NORMA   (*turning swiftly back*) Oh, Maggie, Tom, has anyone telephoned for me?

MAGGIE   Have you checked your pigeonhole?

NORMA   Of course. Only a Christmas card from a dear old fan. (*Beat.*) Must have just arrived. I took out oodles just before we went up.

TOM   Were you expecting anyone # in particular, Norma?

NORMA   Just Gerry and the girls. They'll probably call later when they know we've come down. Nothing to worry about. Well, must track poor dear Bernard. (*As if vouchsafing a state secret.*) Did you know the Variety Club once named an entire Sunshine bus after him? (*A significant glance, and then she is gone.*)

                   (*Beat.*)

TOM   (*to* MAGGIE) Not a word about failing MOTs.

MAGGIE   No, I genuinely feel sorry for the bloke. Nick May in one ear and Norma in the other. No wonder he'd rather talk to the monkey. (*Into tannoy.*) Miss Krabbe, if you're holding our ASM hostage, could we please begin diplomatic talks?

TOM   Poor Norma. Ironic, isn't it? The only people asked to express any real emotion are the likes of Jake and Sally: complete novices who've

never experienced anything vaguely life-
shattering. Then there's Norma and Bernie,
who've seen it all, felt it all, but only get to be
either shallow-stroke-funny or shallow-stroke-
nasty.

MAGGIE   Jake's got the looks, the name and the billing.
          He sells, and that's that. Put on a nice genteel
          little number for Norma Bailey and Bernie
          Bigelow if you're feeling masochistic, Tom.
          Financially, you'd be better off shutting The
          Old Girl for a week to get the LX sorted.

TOM   Well, funny you say that, Mags. Shutting is
          actually a not-too-distant possibility.

MAGGIE   Oh, not those developers again. I thought
          you'd # managed to win the Council round.

TOM   Can't talk about it now, Mags. Got to go touch
          myself up, having first frisked Wilfred for
          heavy clinking objects.

MAGGIE   Let's talk later then. # If you want . . .

TOM   Definitely. (*Beat.*) Wilfred! They absolutely
          love him. An entrance round every night; his
          one exit, another burst. 'Course, it's an old
          trick. As soon as he's out of sight, he just
          slaps the nearest hard surface to make them
          think someone's started to clap.

MAGGIE   Last night, he missed Wendy by a whisker.
          Literally.

TOM   (*reassuringly*) His aim'll improve. (*Beat.*)
          Funny. He hasn't lost that sixth sense; just the
          other five. Hasn't a clue about his lines, have
          you heard? Just # keeps rolling

MAGGIE   I've heard.

TOM   his eyes and shouting, "Is this all there is?"
          (*Laughs; beat.*) Mags, what if it is?

MAGGIE   One minute, Mr Nancarrow.

              (*Blackout.*)

              (*Lights up to reveal* BARNACLE *and* PISTACHIO
              frontstage, frontcloth.)

BARNACLE   Right then, Pistachio. I've found us work at
              last! I've told Alderman Fitzwarren that we're
              experienced sailors.

PISTACHIO   Seasoned sea salts, Bernie!

BARNACLE   That's right. That's why he's made me Captain
              of his ship, the *Saucy Sal*. And you're my first
              mate . . .

PISTACHIO   I'm your only mate, Bernie.

BARNACLE   No, I mean you're my able seaman, right?

PISTACHIO   Well, I haven't had any complaints so far.

BARNACLE   (*a mock reprimand*) Pistachio!

PISTACHIO   (*obviously a catchphrase*) Nuts!

BARNACLE   As far as Fitzwarren's concerned, I'm Captain
              Bernie Barnacle, and you're Seaman Cummings.
              He mustn't find out that we've never been on
              board a ship before.

PISTACHIO   Speak for yourself. I was once the sole
              survivor of a seriously seismic shipwreck.
              (*Beat.*) Do you want me to repeat that?

BARNACLE   (*obviously another catchphrase*) I'd rather
              you didn't. So, the sole survivor of a
              shipwreck. How did you manage that?

PISTACHIO   I missed the boat. Nuts! No, but, Bernie . . .

BARNACLE   Call me Captain.

PISTACHIO   Where you've got your hand, I thought you
              were a Rear Admiral. Especially, as you seem
              quite attached to my privates. Nuts!

BARNACLE	Pistachio!
PISTACHIO	No, sea salted.
BARNACLE	Now, look! Before we meet Fitzwarren, there's a few things you've got to learn. On a ship, the doors are hatches, the floors are decks, the kitchen's a galley and the dining-room's a mess.
PISTACHIO	Well, I'm not cleaning it.
BARNACLE	We've got to pick up the naval lingo, shiver me timbers and scrub me . . .
PISTACHIO	Bulwarks!
BARNACLE	No, it's true. If he finds out we're really landlubbers, we'll be keel-hauled or made to walk the plank . . .
PISTACHIO	Blow me hornpipe!
BARNACLE	That's it, you're getting it now . . .
PISTACHIO	Aye, aye, bust me barnacles, splay me sluicegates, hoist me hosecannon . . .
BARNACLE	Yes, thank you, Pistachio!
PISTACHIO	Nuts!
BARNACLE	Now we've got the lingo, we need some effects.
PISTACHIO	(*to LX box*) Effects, maestro, please!
	(*Immediately, very loud sounds of wind, galloping horses, gunshots, breaking glass, motor horns, steam trains, screams, etc.*)
BARNACLE	(*shouting at the LX box*) Not those kind of effects! (*The sound effects cut out. To* PISTACHIO.) Belongings, provisions . . .
PISTACHIO	Oh, right. Well, for starters, I need some parrot seed.
BARNACLE	Why, have you got a parrot?

PISTACHIO   No, but I wanna grow one. We'll also need
                1000 miles of rope.

BARNACLE   You mean 'yards'.

PISTACHIO   No, we've got to find our way back.

BARNACLE   Yes, and we'll need some paper to write home.
                Go and ask Sarah at Fitzwarren's Stores if she
                keeps stationery.

PISTACHIO   No, I've heard she wriggles about a bit.

BARNACLE   Pistachio!

PISTACHIO   Nuts!

                (*Instantaneous blackout.*)

Friday 24th December – between the two shows

A spot on SALLY *on the payphone to her mother.* SUZANNE *is
silently warming up to one side, dressed in a skimpy 'medieval
shop assistant' outfit.*

SALLY   I can't wait for tomorrow, Mum. Everyone's
                tearing at the leash. The second show's two
                hours earlier than normal, so the wheel-less
                ones have a chance to make it home via public
                transport. I wish them well. (*Beat.*) Oh, I'm
                just going to do my packing and get an early
                night. Then I'll head off, bright-eyed and
                bushy-tailed, first thing tomorrow, so should
                be with you well before lunchtime. Don't
                expect me to say too much about it though; I
                want to wait till you see it! Oh, Mum, it's
                excruciating. The songs are the worst.
                They've given me 'Raindrops Keep Falling',
                'The Sun Ain't Gonna Shine Anymore' . . .
                Basically, everything weather-related bar 'The
                Thunder and Lightning Polka'.

                (NICK *enters as the light widens to engulf the
                backstage area;* SALLY *sort-of-notices him.*)

Well, all right, Mum. Give Dad and Nathalie my
love. And tell Nats not to open the big one
with the red and green bow until I get there.
(*Beat.*) OK. Bye, Mum. Love you.

(*She hangs up and immediately launches into
a bit of fruit;* NICK *immediately dives into her.*)

NICK   Sal, can I have a word?

SALLY   Of # course, what is it?

NICK   Look, I know Quentin told you to play Alice
                like you are, Sal, but, and I hope you don't
                mind me saying this, I think he's read her
                completely wrong. You don't have to listen to
                him if you don't agree. It's not Quentin who
                has to go out there and make a horse's ass of
                himself. I tell you, Sal, and listen to this
                because it's true and fucking important. Go
                with your gut feeling. Yeah?

SALLY   But I think Quentin's right.

                (*Beat.*)

NICK   Well, if that's your gut feel, Sal, great, go with
                it, let it fly, great. Just wanted you to be sure.

SALLY   I am. 110 percent.

NICK   Great. (*Beat.*) What you doing for Christmas?

SALLY   Driving back to the folks tonight. You?

NICK   Ah, well, likewise-ish.

                (BERNIE *enters from the stage.* SALLY *drifts off
                towards the dressing rooms.*)

                Ah, Bernie, my man, just the guy I wanted to see.

BERNIE   (*pleasantly, as always*) Nick?

PISTACHIO   Prick!

NICK   I wanted to talk to you.

BERNIE   No problem, Nick.

PISTACHIO   Try a psychiatrist. They're paid to listen to shit.

NICK   Do you mind if we cut that line?

BERNIE   Which line?

PISTACHIO   The funny one he keeps fucking up.

NICK   When Idle Jack says, "I've got an 'orrible
            'eadache" and you say, "You need a couple of
            aspirates".

PISTACHIO   (*almost threateningly*) Funny line.

NICK   But do the audience get it?

PISTACHIO   Just because it took you seven rehearsals and
            a visit to Raynes Park Library to get the gag,
            you uneducated shit, don't judge everyone by
            your own standards.

NICK   (*desperately trying to ignore* PISTACHIO) I just
            don't see why I then move downstage to the
            comedy paint ladder?

BERNIE   (*putting a hand over* PISTACHIO'S *mouth;
            laughing*) Well, maybe, Nick, because it's
            funny, it's in the script, and it's what you've
            been told and paid to do, old mate. (*Beat.*) Do
            excuse us. Norma's offering a special recipe
            tonight: Assam with a cinnamon base.
            'Specially for Christmas. (*He goes.*)

PISTACHIO   (*as* BERNIE *takes him off; to* NICK) Drive
            carelessly, cnut features. (*NB: This is not a
            typo.*)

NICK   (*as* BERNIE *and* PISTACHIO *go*) You really ought
            to consider radio, you know. (*Quieter.*)
            Talentless tossers. (*Suddenly seeing* SALLY
            entering, past BERNIE *and* PISTACHIO.) Ah, Sal,
            # great!

SALLY   Suzy, have you seen Jake?

NICK   Shot off in the limo straight after curtain down.
            Didn't even bother to change. I'll be in my
            dressing room if anyone wants me.

            (*He exits, leaving* SUZANNE *and* SALLY *alone.*)

SUZANNE   You're keen on Jake, aren't you.

SALLY   Sorry?

SUZANNE   You fancy him, don't you. You # can tell me.

SALLY   Well, I wouldn't say I # fancy him.

SUZANNE   It's obvious, babe.

SALLY   I have grown to really respect him both # as a
            performer but

SUZANNE   *Respect* him?

SALLY   more as a person. # He's so much more human
            than I thought

SUZANNE   Right.

SALLY   he would be. A genuinely . . . well, genuine #
            guy. I suppose I

SUZANNE   Genuine, sure. You know exactly where you
            stand with Jake.

SALLY   shouldn't have been surprised though. I mean,
            I, as much as anyone, should know that just
            because you're a so-called celebrity, it doesn't
            mean you're not normal. People always # seem
            so surprised when they see me in Tesco's or

SUZANNE   Of course, babe, I know exactly what you mean.

SALLY   in a café somewhere with friends, as if I only
            existed for ninety seconds after each news
            bulletin and then got # put back in my box.

SUZANNE   Like, a few months ago, I starred in this major
            'Crimewatch' reconstruction. Great part.
            Required naturalism, naturally. I was the

victim. And for days after, I kept freaking people out on the street. They thought the poor bitch had been resurrected. (*Beat;* SUZANNE *realises* SALLY *has stopped talking.*) But, anyway, you and Jake . . .

SALLY   Well, as I say, I like him. As a friend # and I think he's really

SUZANNE   Sure. A friend, huh-huh.

SALLY   brought Dick to life . . .

SUZANNE   Oh, yeah, his Dick's amazing.

SALLY   It's just so endearing, # so engaging, so vibrant.

SUZANNE   Well, I certainly can't get enough of it.

SALLY   He just seems to fill that huge space # with his

SUZANNE   He sure does, babe.

SALLY   presence, he's just so alive and # warm.

SUZANNE   Insistent, tireless, oh # yeah.

SALLY   And some of the things he does really tickle me.

SUZANNE   Oh, sure, he makes me scream.

SALLY   I feel quite envious.

SUZANNE   Well, play your cards right, Sal, and I'm sure he'll be able to teach you a trick or two.

SALLY   Actually, Suzy, I was hoping you could. (*Beat.*) I'd like to learn a few moves. (*Beat.*) A few tap steps.

SUZANNE   Oh, right, yeah, sure, whenever, babe. I was going to suggest we should team up, girls together. Take this town by storm. What about after the second show? A few heel-ball-toes and then on to the frozen margaritas. It's Christmas Eve. No show. Just head back home with a stonking hangover.

SALLY	That sounds very nice, Suzy. I'll look forward to that. # Well, not the hangover, of
SUZANNE	So will I, babe.
SALLY	course, but . . .
SUZANNE	On my life.

(*Smiles all around, as the lights fade.*)

(*The lights snap up to full.* DICK, ALICE, JACK, FITZWARREN, SARAH *and* TOMMY *are inside, or just outside, Fitzwarren's Stores, singing the final chorus of a happy, loud, bustling tune. Business is booming. Everything is coming up roses. A big exuberant finish, during which* SUZANNE *comes from the wings and to the fore, then the sound of loud applause. Tableau. Blackout.*)

Sunday 26th December – matinée

As the lights fade up, ROBIN *is waiting backstage, with the usual crossword, but also with* SUZANNE. MAGGIE *and* WENDY *are in prompt corner.*

SUZANNE	So, good Xmas, Robin?
ROBIN	Fair to piddling, Suzy, as my old Dad used to say. You?
SUZANNE	Yeah, cool. Hectic but cool.
WENDY	Wilfred was telling me that he had a marvellous time. Celebrated his sixty-fourth year in 'the biz'.
MAGGIE	Well, I hope 'The Jolly Brewers' have finally chucked him out. I no longer expect presence of mind, but I'm getting pissed off at his absence of body.
SUZANNE	Yeah, would be nice to have the old guy with us this p.m. He called me a different name

every night last week. I wouldn't mind but I'm
supposed to be his favourite sultana.

ROBIN   Still, loves, the old boy does deserve some
           respect. Sixty-four years. That takes stamina.
           It's not the easiest profession to survive in.

MAGGIE   It is if you're barking mad. The easiest.

WENDY   He got his first fan letter just before the
           Christmas Eve matinée. He was crying. I found
           him.

           (*An awkward moment.*)

MAGGIE   OK, pet. Don't set us all off. The state of the
           wiring, we'll short-circuit The Old Girl.

           (NICK *and* BERNIE *enter from the stage.*)

NICK   (*as always, mid-flow*) The thing is, Bernie,
           why is Jack idle? Is it nature or nurture?
           Personally, I think it's the latter. I blame Sarah.
           There's definitely a bit of Oedipus complex #
           going on there.

BERNIE   If you say so, Nick, yes. Hello all.*

ROBIN   Bernie. Good house.

SUZANNE   * Hi.

WENDY   * Oh, Mr Bigelow, I found your custard pies.
           (*She holds up two foam-loaded pies.*) You'd
           left them on the oojamaphlip. You'll need them
           for the comedy cooking scene # with Jack.*

BERNIE   Oh, right, thanks, Wendy. Very kind.

NICK   * And as for Dick, I think there's # definite
           parallels

WENDY   (*being totally ignored by* NICK) Nick, I found
           your custard pies. For the comedy cooking
           scene.

NICK	with Hitler. The resistible rise and all that. I've studied this, you know, and you can definitely see where the author's coming from.
BERNIE	You know, Nick, I'd like to go hunting with you sometime.
NICK	Sorry, Bernie, anti-blood sports. Anyway, excuse me, must see Sally. (*Heading off to the dressing rooms, straight past* SUZANNE, *and again completely ignoring* WENDY.) I don't know what she was doing with her voice in the 'business is booming' scene, but if she doesn't look out, she'll cut it to ribbons. (*As he goes, he passes* TOM *who enters, clutching a glossy folder.*)
TOM	All right there, Nick? # Good Christmas?
	(*But* NICK *has gone.*)
ROBIN	(*to* SUZANNE) I never bothered with drama school. Straight into rep, like old Dad. Learnt more, plus *they* paid *you*. I remember my # West End début. Crappy little thriller . . . (*He dries up, as* WENDY *passes him.*)
WENDY	(*bursting into tears, and running off*) Sorry, Maggie, # back ASAP.
TOM	(*as* WENDY *passes him*) Hello, Wendy. Good Christmas?
	(*But* WENDY *has gone.*)
	Third time lucky. (*With forced bonhomie.*) Maggie, good Christmas? How's Paul?
MAGGIE	Not bad. Not good, but not bad. Starting to scratch that seven year itch. (*She sneezes.*)
OTHERS	Bless # you.
MAGGIE	Thanks.
ROBIN	It's these corridors.

TOM	(*just before he becomes engrossed in the folder*) Sorry, Robin, but I can only afford to heat the audience.
BERNIE	Half the chorus are going down with pneumonia, aren't they, Suzy?
SUZANNE	(*apparently not having heard*) Sorry, Bernie, going down on who?
MAGGIE	I'm fine, stop fussing.
	(NORMA *enters.*)
NORMA	Hello, darlings. Is Wendy all right?*
MAGGIE	Yes, fine.
TOM	* Not sure, Norma.
ROBIN	* Who, old love?
SUZANNE	* Don't know.
BERNIE	* A bit tearful, I think.
NORMA	Nick?*
BERNIE	I think so.
MAGGIE	* Uh-huh.
ROBIN	* Who, old love?
TOM	* Not sure.
SUZANNE	* Christ knows why. # Better off without.
NORMA	Oh, dear. Poor thing. Maggie darling, was there any post for me?
MAGGIE	Have you looked in your hole?
SUZANNE	There won't be. It's Boxing Day.
NORMA	Oh, well. Just waiting for the next script. I'm expecting a bit of a bumper episode. Thought I could start work on it between the shows.

Never mind. Probably sent it chez nous.
(*Beat.*) Bernard, I've just put the Rowenta on.

BERNIE   (*getting up and following her off*) Oh,
              marvellous, thank you, # Norma.

NORMA   It's orange pekoe.

BERNIE   Absolutely smashing. I've brought some
              home-baked shortbreads, as threatened.

NORMA   (*as she exits*) Oh, you shouldn't have,
              Bernard.

PISTACHIO   (*to* BERNIE, *as they exit after her*) You really
              shouldn't.

ROBIN   (*to* SUZANNE) Good old Bernie. One of the old
              school. Been there, done that, got the poster
              in the loo. What a CV he must have.

SUZANNE   (*suddenly*) Wanna hear mine? *

MAGGIE   No. (*Heading off.*) I'm going to see how
              Wendy is.

ROBIN   * Well, I think I've seen it in the prog, old love.

              (TOM *is engrossed in his folder.*)

SUZANNE   (*reciting rapidly by rote, hardly pausing for
              breath*) Suzanne took her first theatrical steps
              at the Doreen Jarvis Academy of Dance.
              Subsequently, she has starred as Liesl in 'The
              Sound of Music' at the Embassy, Skegness,
              enjoyed an engagement in 'Cats' in Hamburg,
              understudied major roles in the Texaco national
              tour of 'Salad Days', and was thrilled to appear
              in a Royal Variety show, in the presence of the
              Duchess of Kent and the former Secretary of
              State for Agriculture. She has featured in
              several summer spectaculars at the North Pier,
              Blackpool, and starred in a number of pop
              videos, fashion and hair shows, and one TV ad
              for Saga Holidays. She recently made her

London West End début as Second
Cheesegrater in 'Beauty and the Beast'. (*Beat.*)
Fucking impressive, not?

ROBIN   (*Looking up from his crossword*) Suzanne
Brett. I've just realised, it's a deliberate gag.
'Soubrette': a pert, coquettish maid servant.

SUZANNE   Spot on, Robin. I may be from Doreen Jarvis's
in Southend, but I'm not a complete twat.
Margot Fonteyn was born Peggy Hookham,
Judy Garland: Frances Gumm, and Doris Day
was really Doris van Kappellcrap or such like,
so why shouldn't Julie Rowbottom have an
upgrade?

ROBIN   You've the makings of a great crosswordeteer.

                 (JAKE *enters from the stage.*)

SUZANNE   I prefer more active pursuits, Robin.

JAKE   Why do I keep having to go on about how
brilliant London is? I know it is. That's why
I'm so pissed off I had to leave it this morning
and come back here.

SUZANNE   (*very close to* JAKE) As we're both here, how
about a last one for the road, Dick?

JAKE   (*after a beat*) Yeah, OK, give me two.

SUZANNE   At least.

                 (*A look, then he goes.*)

                 (*before exiting after him*) Well, Robin, here's
to the good old days. Wish me luck with my
comeback! (*And she has gone.*)

ROBIN   (*to* TOM) Nice girl. She'll go far.

TOM   Well, that's a non sequitur if ever I heard one.

                 (MAGGIE *returns to the wings, as* ROBIN *returns
to his paper.*)

(*to* MAGGIE) Wendy OK?

MAGGIE   Licking her wounds but not purring. (*Seeing the folder.*) News?

TOM   The rats are definitely going for a take-over. (*Passing it to her.*) A ream of gloss showing how The Old Girl could "fulfil her potential". 'The Georgian Journey' no less: "a complete, multi-media experience, combining virtual reality with state-of-the-art puppetronics and genuine factual history". And of course there's the corporate entertainment facilities, oh, and a coffee shop for the plebs.

MAGGIE   Well, at least they've realised she's Georgian.

TOM   Built by John Paty, disciple of Vanbrugh and Wren. (*Beat.*) As Robin has no doubt told you, # this used

MAGGIE   Several times no doubt.

TOM   to be only one of three theatres here. There was the rep, the variety and the touring house. Now there's just the one: The Old Girl. And the ignorant bastards want to gnaw away # at her, too.

MAGGIE   Shush, Tom, no one's listening.

ROBIN   (*looking up*) Sorry?

TOM   Point made and taken.

           (*Beat.*)

MAGGIE   What was it like after Barry went?

TOM   The Old Girl?

MAGGIE   No, life, you fool.

TOM   Well, the mornings are the worst. (*As matter-of-fact as possible.*) Waking up, reaching out, then suddenly remembering and losing him all over again. (*Beat.*) Why?

MAGGIE   No reason.

ROBIN   (*to himself, as he studies the crossword*) I'm
                sure that "gangrene"'s wrong.

TOM   I doubt it.

                (*Lights fade.*)

                (*The lights rise to reveal Highgate Hill:
                foliage, greenery, London hazy in the
                distance, a milestone reading "5 miles to
                London".* DICK, *alone and despondent, having
                just finished a sad song.*)

DICK   (*to audience*) Well, here I am. Highgate Hill.
                Five miles from London Town. You know, kids,
                I trod this very same road only two days ago.
                You probably recognise the scenery. But then,
                although I was as hungry and tired as I am
                now, at least then I was filled with joy and
                optimism. Now, at this very moment, I'm
                hungry, tired, unloved and on the run from the
                police. A boy banned. Still at least I managed
                to smuggle myself out of London via that
                downbeat ballad. (*He sighs deeply, as indeed
                he continues to do for most of the first part of
                this scene.*) Everything looked to be going so
                well. The Alderman told me I'd go far. I didn't
                realise I'd be starting out so soon. If only I
                knew who put Alderman Fitzwarren's money in
                my bag! Now everyone thinks I'm a thief.
                Except for Alice. And Tommy. Where are they
                both? (*No doubt another sigh.*) How beautiful
                London looks from here. I wonder if I'll ever
                see it again? Oh, kids, I've always loved life,
                but I'm beginning to fear it's unrequited.

                (*There is a sudden rustling in the
                undergrowth.*)

                Who's there? It's no good thinking you're
                going to rob me. I've no money. Come on out!
                I'm not afraid of anything or anybody!

(TOMMY *springs onto the stage.*)

Or any cat! (*Realising.*) Cat! Tommy!!!

(TOMMY *'meows' and runs at* DICK, *knocking him flat, and sitting on him, trying to kiss him. Laughing,* DICK *tries to push him off.*)

Stop it, Tommy, get off me! (*Indicating audience.*) Behave yourself; we've got company!

(*Finally,* DICK *manages to get* TOMMY *off him; they sit side by side,* DICK'S *arm around* TOMMY.)

Oh, Tommy, I'm so glad you've found me. I looked everywhere for you before I left. I thought I'd never see you again. You or Alice!

(TOMMY *looks at* DICK *sympathetically.*)

Oh, Tommy. From the very first sight, I had such a soft spot for her. And, you know, Tommy, it just kept getting harder all the time.

(TOMMY *nods sympathetically.*)

And now, I'll never see her again.

(TOMMY *shakes his head.*)

Oh, it's true, Tommy. Abandon hope. Pandora took the money. (*NB: This is supposed to be a gag and not a reference to who put* FITZWARREN'S *cash in* DICK'S *bag!*)

(TOMMY *makes 'going to sleep' actions: head laying on paws, etc.*)

Are you tired, Tommy?

(TOMMY *nods his head.*)

Yes, it has been a hectic day, hasn't it. Well, good night, old friend.

(TOMMY *curls up beside* DICK.)

Yes, that's it, sleep! And then perchance to dream. At least, in dreams, we can be happy, and I can be with Alice.

(TOMMY *once more makes 'sleep' actions.*)

Yes, good night. (*He curls up, closing his eyes.*) Tomorrow is another day. Though, Tommy, at this very moment, quite frankly I don't give a damn.

(TOMMY *raises his head and eyebrows, and then lies down once more. Softly, the lights dim and magical music is heard.*)

Thursday 30th December – second performance

The lights rise to reveal ANASTASIA *and* WENDY *in the former's dressing room.*

ANASTASIA	(*pouring herself a not-so-small vodka*) Well, it is simply not good enough.
WENDY	I'll have another hunt in the interval, Miss Krabbe. A really, really serious look. But we've got to go on in two minutes.
ANASTASIA	Da, I must go on, missing a bell. I will be the Fairy of the Bell. Singular.
WENDY	Oh, you've got plenty more. One won't show from the front, honest.
ANASTASIA	It is the missing piece that mars the picture. (*Indicating herself in the mirror.*) Look! It requires total commitment to create and preserve utter perfection. Commitment, touch-ups and tuck-ups. Not forgetting make-up.

(*Adding a little more, perhaps.*) I should be sponsored by Dulux.

WENDY   You are funny.

ANASTASIA   And you are a fool. I am tragic. My fourth husband, God rot his ashes, said I made Camille look like Pollyanna.

WENDY   Your fourth. (*Thinking hard.*) Now that would have been, golly, now let me see . . .

ANASTASIA   Let me guess. It will be quicker. Patrick Fleming.

WENDY   Oh, that's right! # Oh, Daddy says he

ANASTASIA   Thank you.

WENDY   was a genius.

ANASTASIA   He was a bastard. A self-obsessed, neurotic, sex-crazed schizophrenic with image and alcohol problems. After only two years, we divorced. Irreconcilable similarities. (*Beat.*) Glad he is not here to see this: the final degradation.

WENDY   Oh, but it's not. It's truly not. Everyone absolutely adores you.

ANASTASIA   I hope Daddy can afford to buy you a flower shop, because you will never make it as an actress. They do not love me back here. They no longer love me out there. Fact. Where are the fan letters and autograph seekers at the door, the flowers and champagne in the interval, the invitations to dinner and dalliance after? Ah, à la recherche du temps perdu.

WENDY   But it's a brilliant audience tonight. The best we could want for the final show of the year. It's positively packed.

ANASTASIA   Ah! I knew there was someone out there. I could hear them coughing.

WENDY   I'm only sad it means we're nearly halfway
               through.

ANASTASIA   How comforting. To turn the corner. To return
               to civilisation. To leave this retarded turdhole.

WENDY   Oh, it's really rather sweet, really. We actually
               only live about ten miles away, inland, where
               it's more countrysidey. When you get to know
               it, it's a rather super # place actually . . .

ANASTASIA   (*finally losing it*) Well, I do not wish to get to
               know it. I wish I had never come. I do not
               know why they asked me to come. All I get is
               second billing and fifteen minutes' stage time
               in a three hour show. And I do not even get
               Dressing Room Number One in which to spend
               the other two and three-quarter hours. All I get
               is disrespect, incompetence and aggravation
               before, during and after the interval. And you,
               with your shit-eating smile! I do not need to
               go down to the fucking prom to hear the sea. I
               only need to stand next to you!

               (*Beat.*)

WENDY   (*with a shit-eating smile*) Well, I suppose
               we're all a bit excited about the break.

               (*Blackout.*)

               (*The lights rise to reveal once more Highgate
               Hill.* DICK *and* TOMMY *are asleep on the
               ground. Dim lights and magical music. Then*
               FAIRY BOWBELLS *appears.*)

BOWBELLS   Hello again! 'Fraid I can't stop for long.
               But I've just heard all Dick's plans have gone
                                                    wrong.
               A little bell told me. What a clanger!
               Still, I suppose you need a cliffhanger.
               Dear Dick, your wish will soon be granted;
               The Bells of London Town I have enchanted,
               And now they peel from ev'ry steeple tall!

Harken to their message. Hear their distant call!

(*And indeed the sound of distant bells can be
heard.*)

(*Singing to the tune of 'Oranges and Lemons',
accompanied by an offstage chorus.*) Turn
                                again, Whittington,
Fortune awaits you. #
(*To audience, of offstage fellow actors.*) Well,
                                they've all had their

CHORUS   (*continuing to sing under the following
                    dialogue*) Come back to London
                                And you'll be Lord Mayor.
                                Come back! Good fortune
                                Awaits you in London.
                    (*Joined by* BOWBELLS, *after the dialogue.*) Sir
                                Richard Whittington,
                                Three time Lord May'r.

BOWBELLS   chance to carouse!
                    Besides it's a nice way from sleep Dick to
                                                        rouse!

DICK   (*waking with a start*) Tommy! Listen! It's the
                    bells of distant London Town. All ringing
                    together. What are they saying?

BOWBELLS   (*joining in the final couplet with the offstage
                    chorus*) Sir Richard Whittington,
                                Three time Lord May'r.

                    (TOMMY *is now wide awake, too.*)

DICK   'Tis but a dream! But Tom, I could have sworn
                    That on the air a foreign voice was borne,
                    Which bade me "turn again", and not despair,
                    Promising I should thrice be made Lord Mayor.
                    'Twas but a cruel fantasy . . .

BOWBELLS   (*appearing to him*)   Oh, no!
                    Dick, listen to the chiming Bells of Bow.
                    Hark to them and you shall hear quite plain,
                    "Turn, Dick Whittington, turn and turn again!"

DICK   (*amazed*) Who are you, dear strange and
                                         lovely vision,
                With a voice as golden as Eurovision?

BOWBELLS   Fairy Bowbells, dear, and pressed for time
                So, if you don't mind, leave me to do the rhyme.

DICK   Tommy, I must be dreaming.

BOWBELLS   This is Highgate Hill, dear, not Kansas.
                And you shouldn't be out here. At least with
                                         no canvas.
                Dick, fortune is smiling, you must catch the tide.
                Turn back, or not, it's for you to decide.

DICK   But, Fairy Bowbells, how could a poor country
                boy like me ever become Lord Mayor of
                London? And three times! It's impossible.
                And yet, you're really there. I can see you.
                And the bells really rung. I heard them.
                Perhaps I should take courage from you, and
                return. After all, only the earth shall inherit the
                meek. Tommy, what do you think? Should I go
                back?

                (TOMMY *nods ferociously, encouraging the
                audience to do so as well.*)

                (*to audience*) What do *you* think? Should I go
                back? Should I? (*That seems to have decided
                it!*) Yes, you're right! Thank you all! You
                never get anywhere if you run away from
                everything. If nobody loves you when you're
                down and out, I'll prove they do when you're
                up and in. (*To* FAIRY BOWBELLS.) Thank you,
                Fairy Bowbells! I will not let you down. I will
                return to London, to clear my name and make
                my fortune. Come on, Tommy, race you down
                the hill!

                (*And off* DICK *and* TOMMY *charge, waving
                goodbye to both* FAIRY BOWBELLS *and the
                audience.*)

BOWBELLS   There goes brave Dick, straight to London's
                                              Guildhall;
              As happy as Cinders on her way to the ball.
              Such scenes make me want to croon and swoon.
              But can't stop! Got to give Jack's beanstalk a
                                              prune.
              Then after that, well, my workload redoubles:
              You see, Snow White's got . . . a few little
                                              troubles.
              No wonder I'm hooked on elfin caffeine!
              Well, must dash, now it seems I've finished the
                                              scene!

              (*Blackout.*)

Thursday 30th December – after the evening performance

The lights find TOM *alone on an empty stage, staring into the
auditorium. The working lights are on.* TOM *is for once in
'day' clothes, not dressed as* SARAH. *After a second,* MAGGIE
enters.

MAGGIE   Tom, you all right?

TOM   (*roused*) Oh, yeah, sure. Just checking the
              house.

MAGGIE   I thought you did that during Sarah's first
              monologue.

TOM   No, that's when I *count* the house. Everyone
              gone?

MAGGIE   Yes. It was like the end of term back there.
              The likes of Robin, Norma and Anastasia, their
              feet didn't touch the floor, but the youngsters
              have been clinging on as if they'd never see
              one another again. Silly sods are back in sixty
              hours. (*She sneezes.*)

TOM   Bless you.

MAGGIE   Thank you.

TOM   Another year. Another mixed bag of mixed-up
              has-beens, wannabes, never-will-bes and why-
              ever-were-theys.

MAGGIE   You said it.

TOM   God, I love 'em.

MAGGIE   I'll love the break.

TOM   You and Paul up to anything special?

MAGGIE   Well, we've nothing much planned, but he's
              been very secretive lately. I think he might be
              working up to a proposal # of sorts.

TOM   Oh, Mags, fingers # crossed.

MAGGIE   Well, I've given him more prompts than
              Wilfred. Where do you pick 'em?

TOM   Wilfred? He's a national treasure. # Everyone
              keeps asking me where I dug him up.

MAGGIE   Everyone keeps asking you where you dug him
              up.

              (*A shared laugh perhaps.*)

              I must hand it to you though, Tom. You've
              certainly pushed the boat out on this one.
              Star-studded. It's none of my business but,
              what the hell, how can you afford them?

TOM   They all come a lot cheaper than you'd
              imagine.

MAGGIE   In my experience, people normally do.

TOM   Barry always used to laugh at the way we billed
              people: TV's this, TV's that, so-and-so from
              TV's 'and the other'. (*Beat.*) We never did
              much telly. Barry used to joke that we should

bill ourselves simply as 'Nelson & Nancarrow. TVs. Full stop'.

MAGGIE   You should do telly. It's where the money is.

TOM   Well, it sure as Hell ain't here. We can't survive for the whole year on a five-week panto season, Mags. Still, the writing's been on the wall since I first came. We used to go round all the local shops borrowing props.

MAGGIE   Before my time.

TOM   (*not hearing her*) Can't just do that any more. The locals are all branches of nationals. Ask if they can lend something and they have to refer to Head Office. And Head Office have, of course, already spent the sponsorship budget for this year and the next on some high-profile event with TV coverage. Or, at the very least, fireworks and picnic hampers.

MAGGIE   So, are *we* going out with a bang?

TOM   No, Mags, I'm going to fight every inch of the way.

MAGGIE   But is # it really worth . . .

TOM   But, if I lose, at least we'll have gone out on a high. As you say, star-studded, if of a lesser galaxy. Look at Jake, our star stud himself. Hasn't had a Number Twenty hit for over two years. Suzanne told me his last award was a year ago: Smash Hits' Best Haircut of '99. (*Obviously please change the year as appropriate!*) # I'm beginning to

MAGGIE   She would.

TOM   think all the fans and lust letters come courtesy of his agent. I've started to spot the same faces and handwriting. (*Beat.*) But still, he does pull in the genuine punters. Barry once told me that when the touring companies

finished their run, virtually the whole town
turned up at the station to wave them off. (*As
lightly as possible.*) Theatre was their lifeline.
We can recapture that . . . surely.

MAGGIE   Maybe we can, but it's too late to discuss it
now, Tom. (*Beat.*) What has got into you, pet?
Come on, lighten up. Be the Tom I know. It's
New Year for fuck's sake. How are you
spending the over-hyped hiatus?

TOM   Oh, I've been invited over by an old friend
from uni. Just got married. Wife's expecting.

MAGGIE   Aren't we all? Well, anyway, you have fun.
And forget about this poxy place. Promise me?

TOM   Promise.

MAGGIE   And if you get bored, give me a call. Promise?
You'll

TOM   Promise.

MAGGIE   be more than welcome.

TOM   Promise?

MAGGIE   Besides, Paul'll be glad of a change of voice.
(*Kissing him.*) So, remember, if you're not
enjoying it with your uni friend and his
expecting wife, pop over, and let me completely
fuck it up. (*As she leaves.*) Take care,
sweetheart. Don't stay long, and hit the
workers when you do go. Oh, and if you see
Keith, run for your life, he's a ghost.

           (*MAGGIE has gone. Silence.* TOM *looks out
           into the auditorium once more.*)

TOM   There's only one ghost here, eh, Barry? Don't
worry, my love, I won't let the rats take over.
The Old Girl will see the end of this century,
and the one after that. We just need to rally
the troops, stir up that old sense of civic pride.

I'll get the sodding sponsorship somehow.
We'll fight them on their own ground: in the
video shops, down the cable and on the net.
We'll provide the complete leisure experience,
the ultimate journey! Great theatre, plus full
air-con, free parking, 'à la carte' dining and
top-of-the-range corporate packages: the full
monty. We just need a tiny seed and then we'll
grow. Good God, Barry, this has got to be a
brilliant business opportunity for some
modern-day Whittington. Leaving us to say
what we've always said, to each person out
there in the dark: "This is for you alone. It is
unique. No other, whether they came
yesterday, come tomorrow or catch it in
Clacton, will see, hear or experience quite what
you do tonight. Like a surprise celebration,
planned and executed with such meticulous
care as to appear effortless, this has been made
only tonight, and for you only, and for this
night only. It is very, very special". (*Beat.*) I
won't let them ruin what you gave your entire
life to. (*Beat.*) It's funny, all the things you
never get around to saying. You mean to, but
it never seems to be the right moment, or you
can't find the right words, and then it's too
late, and you realise that any words would
have been better than none. (*Beat.*) Still, no
point saying it now. I'll just show you. We
will not go out with a bang. We will stay.
Promise. We will entertain, enlighten and
illuminate. We will sparkle! Happy New Year,
Old Girl. (*With a flourish, he turns off the
workers. Sparks, a bang, in the blackout.*)
Oh, fuck it!

ACT TWO

To the obligatory accompaniment of thunder and lightning,
QUEEN RAT *appears before the frontcloth. It is the opening of*
Act Two of 'Dick Whittington'.

QUEEN RAT   Welcome back, kiddies. Hope you choked on
                  your lollies.
         Whilst you were gone, I've been cursing my
                    follies.
         Oh, I've been far too kind to that young blue-
                   eyed Dick
         And to his rat-catching feline sidekick.
         No more Mrs Nice Rat! The claws are out and
                   sharp.
         Soon Dick on a cloud will be strumming a harp!
         In my smelly sewer, I've sat and schemed:
         Foul fortunes for Dick in my brain have teemed.
         I've worked out a strategy with spite and guile.
         Oh, how I love being utterly vile!
         Yes, hiss and boo, then jeer some more!
         But the *Saucy Sal* will never see shore!
         On that ship, I hereby place a mocker;
         Soon Dick'll be lying in Davy Jones' locker.
         Blow, winds, and crack your cheeks! Rage! Blow!
         You cataracts, and hurricanoes, spout
         Till you have drenched their topsails, drowned
                  the cocks!
         You sulphurous and thought-executing fires,
         Vaunt-curriers of oak-cleaving thunderbolts,
         Strike flat the thick rotundity o' their world!
         (*Calming down.*) But until the time comes thus
                  to seal Dick's fate,
         In my grisly gutter, I'll watch and wait!

         (*And with the obligatory evil cackle, she*
         vanishes, as does her light.)

Sunday 2nd January – matinée

The lights rise to find TOM, *as usual in his* SARAH *outfit, and*
MAGGIE, *as usual by prompt corner.*

MAGGIE   (*into the tannoy*) Possibly a little heavy on the green, pet.

TOM   (*to* MAGGIE) Tell him she looks positively radioactive.

MAGGIE   (*into tannoy*) I think what we're saying back here is 'less Sizewell'.

TOM   (*to* MAGGIE) The box obviously had a blinding Hogmanay. (*Beat.*) Yours good, Mags?

MAGGIE   Oh, fine. Went to a party and lost Paul at about ten, so can't complain. You?

TOM   Oh, great fun, splendid time. Can't really remember it. # How's the cold?

MAGGIE   Lucky you. Oh, pretty much cleared up, thanks. I think I'm allergic to theatre. Any news?

TOM   Not as yet. (*Beat.*) Was your New Year *really* fine?

MAGGIE   No. Piss-poor. Yours?

TOM   Oh, unreal.

MAGGIE   Imaginary.

TOM   Yeah.

MAGGIE   There wasn't one.

TOM   No.

MAGGIE   Silly sod.

(WENDY *rushes in from the stage in both a state and, as usual, her cat outfit.*)

WENDY   Oh, my God, you'll never guess # what's just happened.*

MAGGIE   What is it? What's happened?

Tom   * What?

Wendy   Bernie's just punched Nick. On stage. In # the
               middle of

Tom   Punched him? # Was it an accident?

Maggie   Oh, Christ alive!

Wendy   their haunted bedroom scene. No, he meant it.
               It wasn't an accident. Nick just played some
               line differently to normal or did something
               funny with his hand, and Pistachio just
               headbutted him.*

Tom   I don't believe it.

Maggie   * So what happened, then? (*To* Tom.) I told
               you there was friction # there. We should have
               moved one of them out of that dressing room. *

Wendy   Well, Nick sort of collapsed, then got up and
               gave Bernie a funny look, then Bernie just cut
               to the end of the scene.

Tom   * Yes, I know. I'm sorry.

               (*They are interrupted by* Bernie, *crossing
               swiftly across the stage, pursued by* Nick,
               clutching a bleeding nose. They are followed
               by a couple of quietly bickering, white-
               sheeted little ghosts.*)

Nick   (*to* Bernie) It's only a fucking play, for #
               Christsake!

Maggie   (*to the disappearing* Bernie) Can I have a
               word, # Bernard?

Tom   (*following after*) Leave it to me.

               (Maggie *and* Wendy *are left alone. Beat.*)

Maggie   (*to* Wendy) Did it get a laugh?

               (*Blackout.*)

Sunday 2nd January – between the shows

NORMA   (*discovered by a spot, on the phone to Gerry;
               the usual cigarette in hand*) So what did the
               doctor say, darling, exactly? (*Pause, then in
               one breath.*) Oh, I said it to you, Gerry, I
               shouldn't be here, I told you, she didn't look
               well all day yesterday, I'm coming straight
               home. (*Beat.*) I know I only came back this
               morning, but they can send the understudy on,
               give her a chance. (*Beat.*) I am not over-
               reacting, Gerald, my baby is ill, she needs me,
               I'm coming. (*Beat.*) I know how old she is,
               Gerry, but she's still my baby. How can I go
               on tonight knowing she's on her own, weak
               and wretched. (*Beat.*) All right, *with you*, weak
               and wretched. I know how she feels, poor
               lamb. I don't think I've ever felt so utterly
               miserable in my entire life, saying goodbye to
               you all this morning. I mean, as I said, the
               hotel's very nice: four crowns and 'Highly
               Commended' by the ETB, but it's not home.
               (*Beat.*) And the hissing's getting worse.
               They've certainly got the hang of this panto
               lark; only wish I had. I truly don't know if I
               can handle stage work anymore. I can't
               remember how to do it. Max was right, bless
               him, start with something trivial and provincial.
               I don't think I could handle a heavy West
               Ender just yet. (*Beat.*) Have the studios tried
               to get me at home today? (*Beat.*) I know it's a
               Sunday, but still . . . (*Beat.*) I'm on the way
               out, Gerry, I know it. (*Beat.*) I do. When did I
               last get a major plotline? (*Beat.*) *I do*: over
               eighteen months ago. When did I last get the
               closing close-up? Nearly three years ago. The
               only time you see me now is for the odd line, in
               the pub or in the shop. In the background and
               in passing wherever. If I'm very lucky I get to
               interrupt someone else's important scene.
               Briefly. Normally one of the youngsters. It's
               why they could so easily let me have these

seven weeks off. A convenient trip to some
sister in Sydney who funnily enough I've never
mentioned in thirteen years! I give them four
months before I read I haven't been able to
settle and have decided to emigrate. I'll
probably get to mention it in passing. Though
they may give me the closing CU as I climb into
the cab. Naturally, the irony'll be lost on them.
(*Beat.*) I'm glad Annabel and Lucy have never
had any desire to don the motley. I wouldn't
wish that on anybody. (*Pause.*) Well, all right,
I'll stay here until my next day off, if you think
Annabel will be OK without me, darling. (*Beat.*)
Give the girls my love.

(*She hangs up, pops a pill into her mouth,
swallows it, inhales her cigarette; all whilst
staring straight ahead, almost without
expression. Slow fade.*)

(*The lights rise on* BARNACLE *and* PISTACHIO *on
board the* Saucy Sal.)

BARNACLE   Well, here we are, Pistachio, safely stowed
            aship the *Saucy Sal*, set to sail the seven seas.

PISTACHIO   Do you want me to say that?

BARNACLE   I'd rather you didn't.

PISTACHIO   So, where are we bound for, batter me bilgepipes?

BARNACLE   Morocco, to see the swarthy Sultan and stock
            up on silks, satins and spices. Don't say it!

PISTACHIO   The Sultan, splice me sidebooms! What'll I say
            to him?

BARNACLE   You must bow low, like this, and say "Salaam,
            salaam".

PISTACHIO   Got it! Salaam, salaam!

BARNACLE   Yes, just think, Pistachio. Morocco! We can
               sunbathe on a white tropical beach, by a clear
               blue sea . . .

PISTACHIO   Browning our furry nuts.

BARNACLE   Pistachio!

PISTACHIO   No, dry roasted.

BARNACLE   Oh, look, the sun's past the yardarm. We
               should be setting sail, but we can't go without
               a crew. Why don't we have a song to pass the
               time? Something nautical.

PISTACHIO   I know a very nautical song. It's called 'She
               Easily Passed for a Sailor, 'Cos She had a
               Sunken Chest'.

BARNACLE   Very naughty-cal! OK. What key are we going
               to sing it in?

PISTACHIO   How about a skeleton key?

BARNACLE   What's that?

PISTACHIO   One that'll fit anything. Nuts!

               (*Blackout.*)

Friday 7th January – matinée

The lights rise to reveal ROBIN *in his dressing room, with*
SUZANNE, *this time in her sailor outfit.*

SUZANNE   I just get so bored with the constant drivel in
               the 'Kids from Fame' dressing room. All CVs
               and ten-by-eights, blow jobs and pipe dreams.
               None of them'll ever make it. As wet behind
               the ears as between the legs. (*Beat.*) Sorry. I
               hope you don't mind me keep coming in here
               seeking refuge.

ROBIN   Not at all, love. Au contraire. You're doing
             wonders for my reputation, if not my blood
             pressure. So anyway, you will make it?

SUZANNE   I think I've a good chance. Probably several.
             And I'm going to grab every one that comes
             along and squeeze # it dry.

ROBIN   Feeling lucky, then, love. Why, d'you get
             pricked by a pin at the cossy fitting?

SUZANNE   I've been pricked enough already.

ROBIN   Most recently by young Mr May.

SUZANNE   (*smiling*) Not too subtle, was he?

ROBIN   I believe he keeps that for the stage.

SUZANNE   It was nothing. Really nothing, believe me. A
             couple of post-rehearsal smash and grabs.
             He's a real hit and run merchant. Which is fine.
             I'm legging it just as fast in the opposite
             direction.

ROBIN   Next panto, maybe he should have a crack at
             Humpty Dumpty. Still, to quote Sarah, "a little
             coitus never hoitus".

SUZANNE   I don't know about that. Before he slammed so
             gallantly into me, he'd been joy-riding with
             poor little Wendy. Almost since the
             readthrough. Seems pretty cut up about it.
             Thought it was the real thing.

ROBIN   Oh dear. Confusing theatre with the real thing.
             She'll get over it. One does. It's part of life.
             Especially our life, all cocooned together in
             this backstage pressure cooker. Got to let the
             air out somehow. I remember my first job
             without Dad. Twice nightly, once weekly rep in
             Musselburgh of all places. I was only
             seventeen. This young girl, terribly pretty,
             played all the ingénue roles, made a beeline.
             I'd only been there a few days and she asked

me out for a drink. When the pub chucked us
out, we stood on the wet pavement, still
chatting away pleasantly. I remember she had
the loveliest eyes: deep, soulful brown, like
Young's Ramrod. Then before I knew it, her
tongue was in my mouth and her hand was in
my crotch. For all I know, might have been the
other way around. We were both very drunk.
For the next three months, I used to carry her
to my room, not out of chivalry but fear the
landlady would hear two sets of steps on the
stairs.

SUZANNE   What happened to her?

ROBIN   God knows. Season ended; she never wrote.
           Now she's probably wedded to a Basingstoke
           accountant and a bottle of gin. (*Beat.*) That's
           one of the few perks of theatre: shared digs.
           Don't get it with telly. You do an episode of
           'The Bill' and then all eff off home.

SUZANNE   As opposed to off home effing.

ROBIN   Quite. Of course, in those days, we had to be
           fast in more ways than one! You arrived in
           some Godforsaken town, got handed half a
           dozen scripts and told to learn 'em by Monday.
           Bloody terrifying. If you can # handle

SUZANNE   I can imagine.

ROBIN   that and all the inevitable cock-ups, my son, no
           audience in the world will ever hold any fear for
           you.

SUZANNE   I don't fear anything.

ROBIN   If you so much as sniff success, love, you will.
           You'll fear the missed opportunity. Not
           keeping yourself free for the mythical telly that
           might come off, sometime soon, maybe, never.
           You can't risk doing 'School for Scandal' in
           Scarborough because you're up for an episode
           of 'Casualty'. Look at your Nicholas # May.

SUZANNE   He's not mine!

ROBIN   I can tell you now: Nicholas May certainly won't.

SUZANNE   Not with me again, at any rate.

ROBIN   Mind you, there were knackers' yards of
           turkeys. We pine for the good old days, but
           conveniently forget the bad old nights.
           Sometimes it was like growing mushrooms: kept
           'em in the dark and fed 'em crap.

SUZANNE   I've spent the last year hopping from one
           technicolour turd to the next. Songs of the era
           shows, catering for the coachloads that might
           find Andrew Lloyd Webber a bit too highbrow.
           Well-known tunes, little known leads and a
           completely unknown chorus, including Yours
           Truly, who do all the legwork and get listed at
           the back of the programme in alphabetical
           order. To sweeten the pill, they give us proper
           Christian names, Sandy, Candy, Brandy, to kid
           us and them we're real characters. And, of
           course, Mandy in 'Crock of Shit' looks better
           on the CV than Chorus or Rockette or Peach
           Lady in 'Crock of Shit'. So we sing and dance
           our bursting little hearts out, all tits, teeth and
           sweat.

           (*Beat.*)

ROBIN   Still, it's live. Don't knock it.

SUZANNE   I can't. It pays the rent. # Almost.

ROBIN   What I love most about live theatre is
           matinées, like these. With people out there
           that really want to be. Not because it looks
           good, or they've got tanked up before or hope
           to get shagged later, but purely because they
           want to be here, focusing their entire
           concentration # *on us.*

SUZANNE   Steady, Robin, you're sounding like Nick.

ROBIN   You know how to wound. (*Beat.*) Out there
today are kids who've never been in a theatre
before in their lives: all eager-eyed and living
every second. And there's the old uns, who
come in the afternoon because they worry
they'll nod off at the evening show. It's a
great responsibility, Suzy, knowing that each
time you walk out on that stage, you are giving
somebody their first ever taste of the wonder
that is theatre. And also someone else their
last. (*Beat.*) When Nick May next asks, love,
tell him *that's* our motivation.

(*Beat.*)

SUZANNE   Robin . . .

(*Before she can continue, there is the sound of
a gun firing in the near distance: six shots in
steady succession. An eerie silence, and then
all hell breaks loose . . .*)

(*The lights come up on the wings and prompt
corner, as* TOM *and* JAKE *drag* BERNIE *from the
stage, through the wings, to the offstage
dressing room.* PISTACHIO, *as always, is on*
BERNIE'S *arm, albeit twisted behind his back.*
TOM *carries a handgun.* BERNIE *is silent. As*
TOM, JAKE, BERNIE *and* PISTACHIO *cross,* MAGGIE
is calling into the tannoy. WENDY *is beside
her, obviously shaken, whilst* NORMA *and*
ANASTASIA *watch on, startled.* ROBIN *and*
SUZANNE *leave the dressing room and join the
action. Pandemonium.*)

TOM   (*to* JAKE) That's # it, keep

JAKE   I thought he was kidding; I saw the gun, but I
thought it was another of his gags. Even when
it went off, I thought it was only caps.

TOM   hold # of him, Jake! Come on, Bernie.

MAGGIE   (*into the tannoy*) Call the police now. Of
              course, it # wasn't

TOM   (*leading* BERNIE *offstage, with* JAKE'S *help*)
              Come on, let's go and have a nice lie down, eh?
              Come on, Bernie, come on. Not shooting with
              the gentry, now, Bernie.

MAGGIE   a fucking prop, you idiot. We've been doing
              this for a month, when did Bernie have a gun
              before? Shut the fuck up and call the police.
              And put a bit of music on to cover. I don't
              care which fucking track, just make it loud and
              lively. And bring the houselights up. We'll
              pretend it's another interval.

              (TOM, JAKE, BERNIE *and* PISTACHIO *are now gone.*)

NORMA   (*to* WENDY)   What happened?

WENDY   Bernie came on for his scene with Nick. With a
              gun. He just started firing it. Well, Pistachio
              did. The monkey did it, he had the gun in his
              mouth. The monkey did it. # He just kept

NORMA   No, you're joking! Oh, how awful. Oh my God!
              Oh my God!

WENDY   firing at Nick and into the audience. Just #
              kept firing.

ANASTASIA   I knew it was not going that well tonight, but
              this is ridiculous.

NORMA   Oh my God! # Oh my God!

WENDY   (*spotting* NICK *who has entered from the stage
              ashen-faced, and rushing to him*) Nick! Nick,
              are you all right?

NICK   Of course I'm not, you silly fucking bitch. That
              mad nutter just fucking shot at me. With a
              monkey.

NORMA   (*rushing to* NICK) Oh, my darling! I always
             said there was something wrong there. I
             always said it. I did, I've been saying since the
             readthrough, when one first met him, # if not
             before.

ANASTASIA   (*to* NICK) Come with me. I have a bottle of vile
             Scotch, but it is better than nothing. If you are
             not in shock now, you will be.

WENDY   I'll come with you.

ANASTASIA   (*leading* NICK *off*) As you know, it is a small
             dressing room. Visit when I return to the
             Palladium.

             (*And so,* TOM *and* JAKE *have dragged* BERNIE
             off, and ANASTASIA *has removed* NICK. *There is
             a silence.* NORMA *lights a cigarette.* WENDY
             looks glum.)

MAGGIE   (*into the tannoy*) Thanks, eagle eyes. Stick
             another Christmas favourite on, would you? If
             the local bill enter front of house, point 'em in
             my direction. If they try and storm the stage,
             they'll be stoned to death with out-of-date
             Mars bars. (*To* WENDY.) Mind the fort, Wendy
             honey. I'm going to try and head the law off at
             the pass door. (*She exits.*)

SUZANNE   Well, lovely to see the fuck-up fairy's paid us
             another unscheduled visit.

             (*Beat.*)

TOM   (*entering, to no one in particular*) Everything's
             dandy. The police are en route. Anyway,
             apparently, they were only blanks.

             (*He sits, in silence.*)

ROBIN   You know, there was this 'Peter Pan' I
             remember, with a wacking big scene set on the
             pirate ship. One show, the flyman was a little
             on the enthusiastic side and the Fairy's wire

twisted with the mast. The poor dear spent the rest of the scene just revolving round and round, saying her lines every time she found herself facing front.

(*Beat, as* TOM *makes himself sort-of-comfortable in prompt corner.*)

NORMA　　　I played Tinkerbell once. At school. Such a lovely role. I was so happy. The editor of the school magazine, Lucy Watkins, said I stole the show: "Endearingly winsome". Tiger Lily said that Lucy fancied me, but I think that was just jealousy.

TOM　　　(*to* WENDY) Don't worry, Wendy. He's an actor. Only firing blanks. (*Beat; his hand on a switch.*) Now, do I press this one for a BO?

(*Blackout.*)

(*The lights snap up to show* DICK, ALICE, JACK, FITZWARREN, TOMMY, BARNACLE *and* PISTACHIO *on board the* Saucy Sal.)

FITZWARREN　　So, all present and correct, Captain Barnacle?

BARNACLE　　I think I'm still one seaman short of a shipful, sir.

PISTACHIO　　We know.

JACK　　Oh, that'll be Mum. I hope she's all right. I just saw a sign "Trips round the harbour. Married men: five pounds. Wives thrown in".

DICK　　Perhaps we should send out a search party.

BARNACLE　　Good idea, sailor. What does she look like?

FITZWARREN　　Much better with your eyes closed.

ALICE　　Blonde hair.

DICK　　Red cheeks.

JACK　　And hazel . . .

PISTACHIO	(*interrupting*) Nuts!
BARNACLE	Pistachio!
JACK	No, there she is!
PISTACHIO	Aye, hand ahoy!
BARNACLE	You mean "land".
PISTACHIO	No, now we've all the hands on deck, biff me bulkheads!
	(SARAH appears.)
ALICE	Oh, Sarah, we were just going to set sail.
DICK	What perfect timing!
PISTACHIO	(*to audience*) He obviously didn't see her last scene.
SARAH	Oh, sorry I'm late, but I've just had a terrible experience! I was followed by this feller. All the way down the street. I walked ever so slowly but he wouldn't catch up. Anyway, eventually, I went up to a policeman and complained. "There's a man following me," I said. "I'm sure he's drunk." Well, the policeman looked me up and down and said, "Yes. I think he must be." (*To audience.*) Don't clap too loudly, it's a very old building.
FITZWARREN	Right, well, now you're here, let's slip anchor.
SARAH	(*coyly*) Oh, Fitzy, not in front of all these people!
BARNACLE	Aye, aye.
PISTACHIO	(*to* FITZWARREN) Salaam, salaam.
BARNACLE	You don't say that to him. He's not the Sultan.
PISTACHIO	Oh! Falsalaam, falsalamm!
BARNACLE	Right, Dick, you batter down the hatches.

DICK	(*running off*) Aye, aye, Captain.
BARNACLE	Jack, up in the crow's nest.
JACK	Where's that?
BARNACLE	Atop the mizzen mast.
JACK	I can't go up the mizzen mast.
BARNACLE	Why not?
JACK	It's mizzen.
BARNACLE	In that case, go to the engine room. You can be the ship's Stoker.
JACK	(*dawdling off*) Aye, aye, Captain.
FITZWARREN	I thought this was a sailing ship. The engine hasn't been invented yet.
BARNACLE	Well, looking for it should keep him out of trouble for quite a while.
ALICE	What can I do, Captain?
BARNACLE	Well, my lady, you could climb up that ladder and unfurl me foresail.
ALICE	(*running off*) Aye, aye, Captain.
FITZWARREN	Be careful, Alice. If you fall off and break both your legs, don't come running to me!
PISTACHIO	What'll I do, spray me seamen?
BARNACLE	No, you don't. Stay close to me. (*To* FITZWARREN.) You see, Alderman, my men would follow me anywhere.
SARAH	But only out of morbid curiosity. (*Beat.*) Oh, Fitzy, I love cruising!
FITZWARREN	You're not here to cruise, Sarah. You're here to work. Things are going to be rough and ready.

SARAH	(*sotto voce*) We've done that one.
FITZWARREN	(*likewise*) Oh, right.
BARNACLE	Are you familiar with the Navy?
SARAH	Not all of them. Though, last week, I did go out with a second lieutenant.
BARNACLE	Why a second lieutenant?
SARAH	The first one got away.
	(*Blackout.*)

Wednesday 12th January – after two days off

A spot reveals SALLY *talking on the payphone.*

SALLY   As I say, Nats, brilliant to see you all. Got back at about eight and went straight out on the town with Suz. Felt like death today. Couldn't even go on this afternoon. It goes without saying, Nats, but don't tell Mum. (*Beat.*) Well, I got a lie-in and poor Suzy got her big chance. It's so unfair after all, Nats; she's a much better Alice than me. Actually, some big West End agent or other was in this p.m. (*Beat.*) Well, if he signs Suzy up, good on her. (*Beat.*) Don't go on, sis. If the man's interested in me, he'll come back, and, yes, I am fighting fit for tonight, thank you, still on a dozen apples a day, so quit worrying. (*Beat.*) No, I'm not "pissing it up with her again tonight", Nats. Well, please, please, don't tell the folks, but . . . Jake's asked me out. (*Beat.*) Well, of course I said 'yes'! I haven't completely lost it.

(*The spot fades rapidly . . .*)

(. . . to be replaced by lights on ANASTASIA'S *dressing room. She and* NORMA *burst in.)*

ANASTASIA   Now, sit down, I pour you a very large vodka. # Do not

NORMA   *(obviously shaken)* Oh, no, not during a performance.

ANASTASIA   argue. It is good for you. Made from potatoes. # What the hell!

NORMA   I dried! All alone out there, just me, that awful green spotlight, and them. I just stared at them. Couldn't remember the words.

ANASTASIA   No doubt they thought it was a highly dramatic pause.

NORMA   But I must have been there for a minute at least.

ANASTASIA   They know you have done Pinter.

NORMA   Not all of them.

ANASTASIA   Well, not even his greatest fan could do all of them. So tedious.

NORMA   No, I mean, not all of them would know of my classical credentials. The hoi polloi probably guessed quite rightly that something was wrong. They're not used to pauses. When they watch me on telly, they expect wall-to-wall waffle. They're lonely, you see. Even if they're sharing a sofa with their loved ones, they're lonely. They need constant chat. *(Beat.)* They knew I dried.

ANASTASIA   Screw them! You are June Gladwell. "One of the greatest comic creations since Dickens", 'The Mail on Sunday' colour supplement.

NORMA   *(rather pleased)* You read that?

ANASTASIA	No, you told me the first time we met. (*Beat.*) Who are they? Sad, lonely nobodies. You've found them, good. Now, fuck 'em and forget 'em, as my fifth husband used to say. Only intelligent conversation I ever got out of the son of a bitch . . .
NORMA	(*warming to* ANASTASIA *and the vodka*) I've only ever dried once before. It was 'The Way of the World', which # as you know is . . .
ANASTASIA	It is another Sunday newspaper.
NORMA	No, it's Congreve. William. # Restoration comedy.
ANASTASIA	I was joking. Never mind.
NORMA	Well, it's terribly complicated, no one ever understands it, but I was going great guns until I got to this particular line and my mind just went a complete and utter blank. Silence. After what seemed a minute or more, there was still no prompt, so I launched into some frightfully frantic ad-libbing. Then, all of a sudden, a voice shouted from prompt corner, "No, try again!" (ANASTASIA *bellows with laughter.*) It was only later I realised the line I'd dried on: "If she should flag in her path I should not fail to prompt her". (*They are now both laughing.*)
ANASTASIA	I am lucky. I have only ever done films.
NORMA	(*without meaning any offence*) Still, you haven't got as many lines as me. And you're not asked for anything deep. # Fairy's all
ANASTASIA	They want me to play Ibsen. In Stockholm.
NORMA	surface. What you give is what they get. I envy you.
ANASTASIA	(*smiling, for once possibly genuinely*) I envy you. Norma, my friend, you have what it takes.

NORMA   (*now quite jolly*) I've probably had it too long.

ANASTASIA   (*laughing heartily, and pouring more vodkas
                 all round*) No, no, pick yourself up, brush
                 yourself off and start all over again. You can
                 do it. You are a mature artist. I never matured;
                 I just got older. When this farce is over, help
                 me with my Ibsen. 'The Lady from the Sea'. I
                 know all about sailors, but I do not #
                 understand her.

NORMA   (*laughing merrily*) As Maggie said, swallowed
                 more seamen than the Bermuda Triangle.

ANASTASIA   Come to me for a holiday. Teach me how to
                 act, all the crying and pacing up and down. I
                 want them to see I am not just a sexy figure and
                 pretty face. You can show me that.

                 (*Beat. They look at each other.* ANASTASIA
                 smiles and toasts NORMA, *as the lights fade.*)

                 (*They rise once more on the* Saucy Sal, *this
                 time to the final chorus of 'We Sail the Ocean
                 Blue', accompanied by a hornpipe dance.
                 This involves* DICK, ALICE, JACK, FITZWARREN,
                 SARAH, TOMMY *and* BARNACLE, *who is for once
                 without* PISTACHIO. *All but* BARNACLE *carry a
                 long mop each.*)

BARNACLE   Right, then, me hearties, form a line. It's time
                 for some drilling!

SARAH   Sounds like fun.

JACK   Drilling? Deep sea? High sea?

BARNACLE   No, I'm not a singer.

JACK   I know. I was standing next to you during the
                 last chorus.

                 (DICK, ALICE *and* TOMMY *are already in line;*
                 JACK, FITZWARREN *and* SARAH *have yet to join
                 them.*)

BARNACLE	Well, get in line! Mr Fitzwarren, Sarah, Stoker Jack!
FITZWARREN	(*looking at* SARAH *with distaste*) I'd rather not.
BARNACLE	No, I mean, get closer.
FITZWARREN	As I said, I'd rather not, but still . . .

(*They are now in a ragged line in the following order:* DICK, TOMMY, ALICE, JACK, SARAH, FITZWARREN; *as they shuffle closer,* JACK *and* ALICE *get trapped. As they struggle to free themselves,* JACK *is pushed out of line; failing to get back in, he rushes to stand next to* FITZWARREN.)

BARNACLE	Right, squad. Number!

(*They all begin to rumba.*)

No, no, no! I said number, not rumba!

DICK	Oh, I see. One.

(*Giggling,* TOMMY *holds up two fingers.*)

ALICE	Three.
SARAH	(*realising that* JACK *was 'number four'*) Five.
FITZWARREN	Six.
JACK	Four.
BARNACLE	Who said that?!
JACK	Who said what?
BARNACLE	Four!

(*They all drop their mops, duck and cover their heads.*)

What are you doing?

JACK	There's some nutter out there playing golf. Didn't you hear him shout "Fore"?

BARNACLE   That wasn't some nutter out there. That was
              me here. As you were, as you were.

              (*They all get to their feet, retrieve their mops
              and return to their original positions.*)

              (*to* SARAH) Right, Sarah, you take Jack's place.
              Go and stand at the end of the line.

              (SARAH *goes to the end of the line, looks at*
              JACK, *then returns to her original position
              without* BARNACLE *noticing.*)

              Now then, from the left, number.

DICK   One.

              (TOMMY *again holds up two fingers.*)

ALICE   Three.

JACK   Four.

SARAH   Five.

BARNACLE   Wait a minute. I thought I told you to stand at
              the end of the line.

SARAH   I did! But when I went, Jack was already there,
              so I came back again.

BARNACLE   Fall out, fall out!

JACK   (*turning on* ALICE) Is that your face or are you
              breaking it in for a bulldog?

FITZWARREN   (*to* SARAH) Drinking suits you, Sarah. It makes
              you look quite beautiful!

SARAH   But I haven't been drinking.

FITZWARREN   I know, but I have!

ALICE   (*to* JACK) Was your mum disappointed? She
              must have wanted children.

SARAH (*to* FITZWARREN) Fitzy, you're not yourself today. I noticed the improvement right away.

(*Meanwhile,* TOMMY *and* DICK *have been silently altercating.*)

DICK (*to* TOMMY) Tommy, I don't know what I'd do without you. But it's fun thinking about it.

BARNACLE (*stopping the others from beginning to tussle*) Stop that! What do you think you're doing?

FITZWARREN You told us to fall out.

BARNACLE Not with each other! As you were!

(*The line straightens again, with* SARAH *taking up position next to* DICK.)

DICK (*to* SARAH) Isn't this fun, Sarah! I feel like a Royal Marine.

SARAH So do I, but where are we going to find one out here?

BARNACLE Forgive me talking whilst you're interrupting, but are you now 'one'?

SARAH Pardon?

BARNACLE I said, "Are you one"?

SARAH Certainly not! But I've an uncle in the Girl Guides we're not sure about.

BARNACLE Oooohhhh! Let's forget the numbers. We'll do some mop drill instead. Atten-shun!

(*They all stand to attention.*)

Crew, present arms!

(*They all rush to him and dump their mops into his arms. He throws them down.*)

No, no, I mean shoulder 'em. Pick 'em up! Pick 'em up!

(*They do.*)

Don't just do something; stand there! Fine. Now, shoulder mops!

(*Everyone lifts their mops with the right hand and transfers them to their left shoulders. The mops of* SARAH, FITZWARREN *and* JACK *shoot over their shoulders and fall. Naturally,* DICK, TOMMY *and* ALICE *complete this manoeuvre correctly.*)

Pick 'em up! Pick 'em up!

(*There is a scramble to collect the mops, involving* SARAH *bending down, her rear to the audience.*)

Avast behind!

SARAH   (*straightening up*) How dare you!

BARNACLE   Look, this is how it should be done! (*He snatches* SARAH'S *mop and performs the manoeuvre.*) Hup, two, three, four! (*He hurls the mop from his shoulder onto the ground in front of* SARAH.) Like that!

ALL   Oh, right. Like that!

                 (SARAH *collects her mop.*)

BARNACLE   Right. Atten-shun! Shoulder mops!

ALL   Hup, two, three, four! (*They repeat* BARNACLE'S *manoeuvre exactly, including hurling the mops onto the deck, beaming happily.*)

BARNACLE   Pick 'em up! Pick 'em up!

                 (*They all retrieve their mops once more.* SARAH'S *mop is between* JACK'S *legs so that as he bends down to pick up his, she grabs hers*)

*and bangs him between the legs. Big comedy
reaction, hopefully with sound effect.*
FITZWARREN *laughs, and* SARAH *swings her mop
to hit him. He ducks, but she completes the
turn and fells him the second time around.
Her turn involves* ALICE, DICK *and* TOMMY *also
ducking.*)

Right, get in line, get in line!

JACK   (*as they get back into line, in the original
order:* DICK, TOMMY, ALICE, JACK, SARAH,
FITZWARREN) Look out there, Mum! Did you
ever see so much water in your whole life?

SARAH   No, son. And we're only looking at the top of it.

BARNACLE   Silence! I'm going to give you one final
chance. We're going to do some marching!
Shoulder mops!

                (*They all put their mops on their left
shoulders, except for* FITZWARREN, *who puts his
on his right.*)

                Not that shoulder! This one! (*He taps his own
left shoulder.*)

                (FITZWARREN *immediately puts his mop on*
BARNACLE'S *left shoulder.* BARNACLE *slaps it
back on* FITZWARREN'S *left shoulder, and moves
away.*)

                Right, left turn!

                (*All turn left, except for* FITZWARREN, *who turns
right.*)

                No, no, turn the other way!

                (*All turn to face the opposite direction.*)

                No, no, as you were! I said 'left'!

FITZWARREN   You said 'right, left'!

BARNACLE   (*wearily*) Oh, it doesn't matter!

                 (*They all put the mops on their left shoulders.
                 JACK's mop goes into SARAH's face and
                 SARAH's goes into FITZWARREN's. SARAH and
                 FITZWARREN make elaborate biz of removing
                 pieces of mop from their mouths.*)

                 Look, the sooner you get marching, the sooner
                 we can all have a nice cool swim.

SARAH   Oh, I daren't. I was once bitten by a crab in a
                 very nasty place.

FITZWARREN   Where?

SARAH   Bognor.

BARNACLE   If you don't concentrate, I'll throw something
                 at you!

SARAH   You could start with my cues.

                 (*They are now back in line, SARAH leaning
                 back at an alarming angle to keep out of the
                 way of JACK's mop, and FITZWARREN doing
                 likewise to keep out of the way of SARAH's.*)

BARNACLE   Straighten up there! Straighten up!

                 (*Reluctantly, SARAH and FITZWARREN do.*)

                 Quick march!

                 (*They all turn left. JACK's mop knocks over
                 SARAH, and SARAH's knocks over FITZWARREN.
                 SARAH hastily pulls down her skirt, which has
                 allowed a pair of very colourful bloomers to
                 show.*)

SARAH   (*getting to her feet*) Oh, you hit me right in me
                 birthmark!

JACK   I didn't know you had a birthmark, Mum.

SARAH   I only got it last night.

FITZWARREN   She climbed into the wrong berth.

SARAH   (*to* FITZWARREN *and* JACK) Ooh, listen to ourselves!

(*The three of them huddle close, in silence, listening to each other intensely.*)

BARNACLE   (*near to tears*) Get back into line. Please . . .

DICK   (*looking skywards*) Oh, look at that huge black storm cloud. It's heading our way.

ALICE   That's funny. The weather forecast was partly sunny, partly windy, and partly accurate.

(*They are now all back in line.*)

BARNACLE   (*having finally lost all patience, and moving to the end of the line, beside* FITZWARREN) That's it, that's it! Crew, down mops!

(*They all bring their mops down smartly,* DICK'S *onto* TOMMY'S *foot,* TOMMY'S *onto* ALICE'S, ALICE'S *onto* JACK'S, JACK'S *onto* SARAH'S, SARAH'S *onto* FITZWARREN'S, *and* FITZWARREN'S *onto* BARNACLE'S. *In unison, they all cry out in pain;* DICK *just smiles innocently at the audience.*)

Nuts!

ALL   Crushed!!!

(*Blackout.*)

Saturday 15th January

The lights rise on the wings to reveal the actors of the previous scene entering from the stage: BERNIE, ROBIN, JAKE, WENDY, SALLY, NICK *and* TOM. MAGGIE *is in prompt corner as per usual.* BERNIE *crosses without a word and exits to his dressing room.*

ROBIN   (*as he crosses the stage behind* BERNIE) Well, I
             think the old mop routine went down very well
             tonight, loves.

NICK   It went down like a bucket of cold sick, love.

             (*But* ROBIN *has already gone.*)

MAGGIE   Jake, Fred on the door's moaning about
             another rainforest you've just had delivered. #
             Could you . . .

JAKE   No problem, Majesty Maggie. (*Exiting.*) I'll
             sort it.

TOM   (*to* MAGGIE) Surprised his agent's wrist hasn't
             ceased up.

SALLY   Pardon? *

TOM   Oh, nothing. (*To* MAGGIE, *exiting.*) Just going
             to check on Bernie.

MAGGIE   * Nothing, pet.

NICK   Sal, we need pepping up. Five mins, your
             dressing room.

SALLY   Sorry, Nick, I'm on again really soon, and must
             call home first. (*Exiting after the others.*) It's
             my kid sister's # birthday.

WENDY   (*to* NICK, *but ignored*) I don't mind # a bit of
             pepping up.

NICK   OK, that's cool. Kid sisters are cool. (*To
             nobody in particular.*) I think maybe I just
             need some quiet chilling out. (*He goes after*
             SALLY.)

MAGGIE   (*to* WENDY) Forget it, love. Definitely not
             worth it. Onwards and upwards, eh?

WENDY	A guy says he wants to see more of you. He seems really nice, so you nod and say, "OK". You think he wants to meet up more frequently. He means he wants to get your kit off, and see all of you.
MAGGIE	They're not all like that, love. Some of them are gay.
TOM	(*entering*) Oh-dear-oh-dear- # oh-dear.
MAGGIE	As if on cue.
TOM	Bernie. Dressing room.
MAGGIE	Good.
TOM	Hitting Pistachio's head on wall.
MAGGIE	Bad.
WENDY	Oh, no, poor thing.
TOM	I know. Bugger's completely flipped.
WENDY	No, Pistachio. He'll hurt him.

(MAGGIE *and* TOM *just look at her. Beat. Blackout.*)

(*The lights rise on* JAKE *and* NICK *in the former's dressing room.*)

NICK	(*very matey*) So, Jake, mate, you're telling me you just saw this ad in the local paper for singers, applied and got signed up.
JAKE	Yeah, but I don't kid myself it was down to my singing.
NICK	'Course not. You're a good looking guy, Jake. Really # fit.
JAKE	Our first record company signed us up before they'd heard a note.

NICK   That's why you can pull any bit of grumble you like.

JAKE   Yeah, well, I dunno, # Nick.

NICK   Have 'em eating out of your lap. Literally.

JAKE   Yeah, well, look, Nick, don't mean to be rude, but I've got to get ready.

NICK   You've aeons yet. Just chill.

JAKE   No, look, mate, # I really must get cracking.

NICK   Not that I don't get my fair share of hole. 'Specially on this show. The totty-tasting's the only thing going for it. (*Listing off his conquests, as* JAKE *begins to make aggravated 'getting ready' actions*.) Little Wendy, Keith's missus, Juicy Lucy, that old slapper in the BJ Bar last week with the sausage tits . . . and, of course, not forgetting Saucy Suzy. Christ, what a filthy cow! Goes like a shithouse door when the plague's in town. But then you'd know about that too, # wouldn't you, Jake, eh?

JAKE   Yeah, well, maybe, Nick, but come on, piss off, eh? I've got to get # my wedding togs on.

NICK   (*making very few 'getting moving' actions*) Yeah, sure. Still, think I've had enough of riding Suze. Too much of a bad thing. But I tell you, Jake, the one I haven't managed to crack open yet: that Sally. # She is

JAKE   Later, Nick.

NICK   something else. Hoity toity totty. I love that sort.

JAKE   She is not a "sort". She's an individual. Remember those, mate? They're what you keep crapping on about # out there.

NICK   Oh, look, mate, no offence, just testing to see if you had a thing going, the two of you.

JAKE   Well, maybe we have.

NICK   And to see if maybe you'd be up for making it a
                "three of us".

                (*Beat.*)

JAKE   (*calling to the bathroom door*) Sally.

                (*The door opens and* SALLY *appears, wearing
                a man's towelling robe.*)

SALLY   Hi, Nick.

NICK   (*taken aback*) Sal.

JAKE   (*calling to the bathroom door*) Suzy.

                (SUZANNE *appears, apparently wearing very
                little, behind* SALLY.)

SUZANNE   Hi, Nick.

                (*Beat.*)

NICK   Four's cool.

                (*Blackout.*)

                (*A spot discovers* MAGGIE *on the payphone,
                obviously talking to an answerphone.*)

MAGGIE   Paul, it's me. Where are you? Down 'The
                Royal George', I suppose. (*Beat.*) Just wanted
                to say sorry about earlier . . . and Christmas
                and New Year and, well, sorry about everything
                basically. It's all beginning to get to me: The
                Old Girl, not having Keith, balancing all the
                egos. Sometimes I feel like I'm running a 'Care
                in the Community' scheme. (*Beat.*) Anyway,
                sweetheart, just wanted to say sorry, not your
                fault, and let's talk later, heh? Or maybe not.
                Just cuddle up with a curry and a bottle of dry
                white. See you soon, angel. Love you. (*She
                hangs up.*)

(TOM *has entered during her call, seen and heard her, and turned to depart tactfully.*)

Tom, did you want me?

TOM	(*turning back*) Eh, yes, Mags, but it can wait. Sorry. Didn't hear much, hardly anything # really.
MAGGIE	That's all right, Tom.
TOM	(*beat*) Domestics?
MAGGIE	Things aren't too good at present.
TOM	Sorry to hear that. You're cold's better though.
MAGGIE	(*smiling*) Yes. Followed my love life out the window.
TOM	Mags, if you need time off to sort this out, # I'm sure I can get cover.
MAGGIE	No, Tom, it's fine. Don't worry. It'll all come out in the wash. What did you want?
TOM	I've got some news. Good news.
MAGGIE	I remember that.
TOM	I heard just before the show went up, so sorry haven't had a chance to tell you before. Now it's too early to get our hopes up, but looks like we might be able to get some Lottery money to keep The Old Girl open. I've got to make further enquiries obviously, but at least it buys us more time. The Council's agreed to put the developers on hold for a while longer.
MAGGIE	How much longer?
TOM	Ah. Don't know. A while. But it's bloody promising, Mags, you've got to admit. # Imagine if we were able to
MAGGIE	Oh, sure, I do.

TOM   buck the national trend. Keep the waves of
             Cool Britannia at bay, here in our own isolated
             little outpost. (*Beat.*) All right, I know, I'm a
             silly Canute.

MAGGIE   I'll reserve judgement a while longer.

             (*The lights crossfade down on the wings . . .*)

             (*. . . and rise on* QUEEN RAT, *who appears
             frontcloth and speaks above the ebbing
             sounds of a shipwreck.*)

QUEEN RAT   I hast performed to point the tempest that I
                                                warned thee.
             To every article.
             I boarded the *Saucy Sal.* Now on the beak,
             Now in the waist, the deck, in every cabin
             I flamed amazement. Sometime I'd divide,
             And burn in many places. On the topmast,
             The yards, and boresprit would I flame distinctly,
             Then meet and join. Jove's lightnings, the
                                                precursors
             O'th'dreadful thunderclaps, more momentary
             And sight-outrunning were not. The fire and
                                                cracks
             Of sulphurous roaring the most mighty Neptune
             Seem to besiege, and make his bold waves
                                                tremble,
             Yea, his dread trident shake. Oh evil spirit!
             Who is so firm, so constant, that this coil
             Would not infect his reason?
             Yes, hear me crow! I shan't be circumspect!
             For the *Saucy Sal* I've well and truly wrecked!
             For our evil, the gods will cherish us . . .
             Oh, do shut up, you little perishers!

             (*Blackout.*)

Sunday 16th January

The lights rise on ANASTASIA'S *dressing room. She is
momentarily alone, possibly pouring vodka, possibly
adjusting her make-up, possibly dosing her one bunch of*

flowers with hairspray. After a second, WENDY *enters in full*
TOMMY *outfit, having cursorily knocked.*

ANASTASIA   (*referring to the flowers*) A single, solitary
                 bunch. I spray them so they last forever. I
                 might as well tilt at windmills.

WENDY   (*with an abrasiveness new to her*) Didn't you
                 hear me tannoying? # We're on in two
                 minutes.

ANASTASIA   Did you not hear me shouting? I cannot go on.
                 Look at me. I resemble a chrysanthemum in a
                 wind tunnel. De-frizz me.

WENDY   I resemble a cat. I am actually a human being.
                 I am certainly not a dog.

ANASTASIA   (*looking at her for the first time*) Are you
                 quoting Beckett or Ionesco? Or is it # Lorca?

WENDY   Oh, shut up. # I am not your

ANASTASIA   I beg your pardon . . .

WENDY   trained poodle, at beck and call, to take your
                 orders and all the rest of your shit. I'm on
                 stage at least five times longer than you,
                 maybe six, plus I've got to help with the calls
                 and the props and the changes, so maybe you
                 should think about helping me out.

ANASTASIA   Do you know who I am?

WENDY   I know who you were.

ANASTASIA   I was a Bond girl.

WENDY   Premium bonds? (*As* ANASTASIA *pours a hasty
                 vodka,* WENDY *pours out her heart.*) More like
                 secondary now. Or maybe even sedentary.
                 See I can use long words too. I'm sick to death
                 being treated like an idiot. My father could
                 sack any one of you like that, but I've never
                 threatened it. I didn't think it would be fair.

But what flipping fairness have I been shown?
The stage crew send me looking for things that
don't exist like a left-handed saw or a black gel
for the lights. I've been touched up by most of
the men who are straight, and the only one I
did let get to me, in all senses, now avoids me
like the plague. # I will no longer . . .

ANASTASIA   I am calling for help. You have Bigelowed.

WENDY   Call away! The only one who ever listens to
                 you is already here.

                 (ANASTASIA *subsides.*)

                 And for the last time. This is the last time I
                 come to give you your call personally, to find
                 your bloody bells, polish your shoes or stitch
                 your tights. From now on, you can blow on
                 your own wet nails, run your own foambath,
                 scrub your own back, and wipe your own
                 fucking nose and bum. (*A parting shot.*) Five
                 weeks ago, I really respected you. It sounds
                 silly but I actually felt honoured to be in your
                 presence. Now, I only feel sorry for you.
                 You're not tragic, you're just sad. You give
                 failures a bad name.

                 (*She has gone. Silence.*)

ANASTASIA   (*to the closed bathroom door*) You might as
                 well come out now. I am no longer in the mood.

                 (*The door opens to reveal* NICK *in his
                 underwear, handcuffed.*)

                 The key is in the cistern.

                 (*Blackout.*)

                 (*Lights up on* SARAH *and* FITZWARREN,
                 *forestage, outside the Stores, both dressed for
                 a wedding.*)

SARAH   Oh, Fitzy, what a difference a play makes! Here
             we are safely returned from Morocco, richer
             than a pair of Lottery winners . . .

FITZWARREN   And almost as rich as a pair of Camelot
             directors.

SARAH   But, Fitzy, money isn't everything.

FITZWARREN   Isn't it?

SARAH   In fact, it's nothing if you're not happy.

FITZWARREN   Well, I don't mind being miserable provided I
             can do it in comfort.

SARAH   (*fluttering her eyelashes*) Better to do it in
             company.

FITZWARREN   Are you feeling all right, Sarah?

SARAH   Never better, Fitzy. We're rich, Dick's about to
             marry Alice, Jack's about to marry the Sultan's
             daughter. Only one thing could make me
             happier.

FITZWARREN   A laugh line?

SARAH   Oh, Fitzy, you know what I mean! (*Flinging
             herself at him.*) Seize the dame!

FITZWARREN   (*extricating himself*) But, Sarah, I'm a very
             eligible bachelor now. I don't want to plunge
             into the first opening that presents itself.

SARAH   Oh, plunge away! As Big Ben said to the
             Tower of Pisa, I've got the time, if you've got
             the inclination . . .

FITZWARREN   After all, I could take a mistress . . .

SARAH   That thing between a mister and a mattress?
             You couldn't!

FITZWARREN   Love can be a very sticky affair, you know,
             Sarah . . .

SARAH   One always hopes so . . .

FITZWARREN   As I told Alice this morning, it's like a
               snowstorm. You never know how long it'll last.

SARAH   True. Or how many inches you'll get. But a
               bird in the hand . . .

FITZWARREN   Does it on the wrist?

SARAH   (*hitting him*) No! Is worth two in the bush, so
               stop beating about it, and propose! I'm as
               legible as you, you know! London's full of
               fellers chasing after me! For a start, there's
               Warren. (*Waving to him, whilst whispering to*
               FITZWARREN.) Sweet man, but a panto short of a
               custard pie, if you know what I mean. The
               sun's rising, but the cock's dead. And then,
               only last month I refused to marry this other
               chap. He's been hitting the bottle ever since.

FITZWARREN   Blimey, that's carrying a celebration a bit far,
               isn't it?

SARAH   (*taking out a large handkerchief, and sobbing
               tragically; without pausing for breath*) You
               brute! All I wanted was a husband, what's left
               of the lover after the nerve's been extracted, all
               I wanted was you, and to make you happy, for
               you to be happy with me, and me with you, and
               us together, to spend our twilight days, as the
               bloom of our youth withers, together, growing
               old gracelessly . . .

FITZWARREN   (*comforting her*) Oh, Sarah, I was only joking . . .

SARAH   (*of audience*) They were wondering when you
               were going to start.

FITZWARREN   Oh, Sarah, dry your mascara.

SARAH   Weddings always make me moist.

FITZWARREN   Then let's make it a triple. Sarah, will you do
              me the honour?

SARAH   Yes, but not until we're married.

FITZWARREN   (*taking her hand solemnly*) What God joins
              together, let no man put asunder.

SARAH   God'll take care of that.

FITZWARREN   Sarah, you've made me the happiest man in the
              whole of London! Apart from Dick and Jack.
              (*An afterthought.*) And Warren.

SARAH   (*to 'Warren'*) Sorry, Warren! But I'll always
              forget you just the way you are.

FITZWARREN   (*ditto*) Yes, sorry, Warren! But, well, I can't
              help myself . . .

SARAH   You can now.

FITZWARREN   After all, she's great around the house, makes
              a lovely stew, and her dumplings are the
              biggest in London.

SARAH   (*simpering happily*) Ooh, flatterer!

              (*Blackout, after possibly a brief song –
              possibly to the tune of 'Here's a how-de-do'
              from 'The Mikado' – culminating in them
              dancing off.*)

Wednesday 19th January

MAGGIE *is discovered backstage, on the payphone to Paul.
She may not be crying at first, but no doubt is by the end.*

MAGGIE   I can't discuss this now, Paul. (*Beat.*) Why?
              Because I'm at work. I'm in the middle of a
              show. Literally. It's the interval. I'll translate:
              it's half time. (*Beat.*) We can't just let it end
              like this. Not after seven years. (*Beat.*) All
              right, six and seven months, you pedantic sod.
              (*Beat.*) Paul, I'm sorry. (*Pause.*) Wait until I'm

back later and let's discuss it. Please. (*Beat.*)
Where can you go? It's all so sudden . . .
(*Beat.*) I see. I should have known. So, how
long's this been going on, she said, sounding
like a cheated wife. Oh, sorry, I said the
unspeakable four-letter word. (*Beat.*) Christ,
Paul, I wish I knew what made you tick. (*Beat.*)
No, I don't wish it was a bomb, you heartless
bastard. Well, you are! I'm the one who
should sound like a bloody panto. You can't
just go like this, Paul. What about the rent, the
cat, the plants, what about me? (*Pause.*) Fine.
Post the keys through the letterbox. You can
phone to arrange a date and time to collect the
rest of your stuff. Or I can just pack it in
binbags and stash them in the garage. You can
keep the key to that. Might be best. Don't
need to see each other that way. (*Beat.*) If you
can check the oil and water on the Renault
while you're there, I'll love you forever. (*Beat.*)
Oh, Christ, Paul . . .

(TOM *enters, with a half-full glass of Scotch.*)

Tom. # What perfect

TOM   Hello, Mags.

MAGGIE   timing.

TOM   Not on yet, surely.

MAGGIE   Oh, no. Haven't even called the three minutes.
           They're still in choc ice and knock-it-back land.
           (*Seeing glass.*) In good company too by the
           look of it. What's up?

TOM   Nothing, Mags, # absolutely bugger none.

MAGGIE   Don't toss with me, Tom. What is it? (*Beat.*)
           You'd better not be getting pissed.

TOM   Well, it ain't cold tea, # Mags.

MAGGIE   Wilfred's one enough. We don't want the
           Saucy Sal swaying one way and you the other.

TOM   Only ever been completely rat-arsed on stage
               once. Been out all day celebrating Barry
               asking me to come in on The Old Girl. We were
               doing Cinders, when weren't we? In the 'scary
               monster, look behind you' scene, he had to
               dash across the stage and leap into my arms.
               Well, I was that pissed, Mags, I saw two
               Nelsons hurtling towards me and didn't have a
               clue which one to catch. (*Beat.*) Picked the
               wrong one, of course. (*Showing* MAGGIE *a
               single sheet with official-looking letterhead.
               Beat.*) The rats have won, Mags. Welcome to
               'The Georgian Journey'! Have a nice day now.

MAGGIE   Oh, Tom. I'm sorry.

TOM   Change is inevitable apparently. Fuckers have
               obviously never used a pub fag machine.

MAGGIE   Tom, I don't # know what to say.

TOM   (*almost oblivious of her*) The only thing that
               matters now, Mags, is money. Today's
               Whittington would have joined the rats. He'd
               be one. Anything to buy up and prise up and
               privatise the pavements of gold. And sod
               society! (*Beat.*) Albert Finney turned down
               'Lawrence of Arabia' to join the Birmingham
               Rep, you know.

MAGGIE   What? One of us has lost the plot # here, Tom.

TOM   Wouldn't happen now.

MAGGIE   It does, Tom, # sometimes.

TOM   It doesn't, Mags. Now, first sign of fame and
               glory, and they're off to Tinseltown.

MAGGIE   They come back.

TOM   Only for a limited run to display their limited
               ability. It's so ironic, Mags, it makes me want

to cry. Where are the Finneys and the Oliviers
of the new millennium going to come from?

MAGGIE   Other avenues, fringed or french-windowed
          perhaps, but it'll still be theatre, for Christsake,
          Tom. # Look, all my

TOM   Not as I know it.

MAGGIE   working life, I've been lectured and hectored
          about the theatre being dead. The lady doth
          protest too much.

TOM   Does she? First Hollywood tore into us like
          Henry VIII into the monasteries, then TV
          banished most of the rest to bingo-dom. Now
          to polish off us last obstinate fuckers still
          clinging to the wreckage, they send the massed
          ranks of the multiplex and the video, # the
          satellite and the net.

MAGGIE   Well, maybe that's where the next Finneys and
          Oliviers are going to come from. Why does
          theatre have to be what you want it to be, just
          because it always has been? We have to
          adapt, Tom, # that's life.

TOM   Adapt or sell out?

MAGGIE   Adapt. We haven't sold out for years, Tom.
          That's why we now have to adapt or die. #
          And if theatre

TOM   Nice wordplay, Mags. Touché.

MAGGIE   does die, it'll be it's own fault, your fault, Tom,
          because as you have said ad nauseum the
          writing's been on the wall for decades. Don't
          you ask yourself why the new Finneys and
          Oliviers choose TV and film, # why the
          audiences

TOM   The money. They're paid a fortune.

MAGGIE   treat live theatre like a leper? # If that's what
          everyone wants, who are you to tell them

TOM   The money. It's too expensive.

MAGGIE   they're wrong? If they've ignored you, then
          start ignoring them.

TOM   So I just sit back?

MAGGIE   Or step forward. If you can't beat 'em, join
          'em. # Go West, young man!

TOM   I don't want to join them, I want to help them.

MAGGIE   They obviously don't want your help.

          (*Beat.*)

TOM   (*a well-rehearsed mantra*) I've always told
          myself that theatre wasn't just a source of
          entertainment, that it was a public service, that
          I personally performed a basic but essential
          social function: bringing people together,
          across all boundaries, # all classes and
          generations . . .

MAGGIE   And satellite, the net and the other two horsemen
          of the apocalypse don't let people do that?

TOM   How can that compare with genuine flesh and
          blood, real sweat and tears really there before
          you, there in the same room, the same space?
          The lights go down, there's a hush, and
          suddenly you're in communion with all these
          strangers, all these souls. Like being in
          church.

MAGGIE   They're only buildings, Tom: shells, cynically,
          deliberately designed to get the ritualistic
          juices flowing.

TOM   Churches or theatres?

MAGGIE   Both. It's no wonder people prefer the telly.
           It's after their minds and souls just the same as
           you, but it doesn't make any bones # about it.

TOM   But what does it want them for?

MAGGIE   What do *you* want them for?

TOM   To gather them together.

MAGGIE   I repeat: and the massed ranks of the multi-
           media don't do that?

TOM   No. They don't. They isolate, they don't
           encompass. # And that's why the

MAGGIE   You're talking crap, Tom, and you know it.

TOM   very concept of community's now dead, Mags.
           I truly believe there's a direct link between all
           this social dysfunction and the death of
           theatre.

MAGGIE   My old nan used to know everyone in her
           street. I bet she never heard of Bernard Shaw
           and never even saw a Shakespeare.

TOM   I'll bet she visited the music hall or the local
           Palace of Varieties.

MAGGIE   Probably. Just as likely as if she was alive
           now, she'd be watching Cilla Black at home
           rather than sitting out there.

TOM   Exactly! At home. Alone. Look at the press-
           ganged youngsters we get in here. No idea
           how to be natural in a group. I should know:
           every night, I can hear the sniggering and the
           sweetpapers. Poor kids today, # they don't get
           frog-marched

MAGGIE   Oh, not the "youth of today" speech. How old
           are you?

TOM   to church like I did, don't eat around the #
             family table.

MAGGIE   What's this obsession with churches? You're
             a bloody agnostic, # for God's sake.

TOM   (*on a roll; not hearing her*) I mean they've
             even killed off the Oxo family for pity's sake.
             They simply don't know how to behave in a
             group, unless it's to pogo up and down to
             music so loud it saves them having to
             communicate!

MAGGIE   Just look in the mirror, Tom! Lamenting the
             demise of great art whilst dressed up like Baby
             Jane.

TOM   Even panto is art!

MAGGIE   What? Now, stop looking, and start listening
             to yourself, Tom. # What did you say?

TOM   Panto is art! It's no different to Shakespeare or
             Shaw or any kind of theatre. # It takes people
             out of

MAGGIE   No, don't listen to yourself. It's bad enough
             one of us has to hear this.

TOM   their own humdrum existences and gives them a
             glimpse of other weird and wonderful worlds.

MAGGIE   A cardboard court of Morocco?

TOM   You know what I mean!

MAGGIE   Obviously not.

TOM   Yes, even panto! Where men are women and
             girls are boys, where the present doesn't just
             acknowledge the past, it embraces it, where
             dreams always come true, and above all, where
             people are hit but never hurt. (*Beat.*) Isn't that
             the most marvellous, marvellous thing, Maggie,
             letting people into that secret, magical garden?

MAGGIE	Sounds terrifyingly familiar, Tom. Straight out of the brochure for 'The Georgian Journey'. And that's also communal.
TOM	Bollocks, that's terminal.
MAGGIE	*This* is the terminal, Tom: The Old Girl. And if there weren't enough travellers ready to switch platforms, the money men would never have bothered you.
TOM	I don't know why I ever bothered.
MAGGIE	I do.
TOM	How the hell do you know what I think?
MAGGIE	Because I know you. I don't understand Paul, I never understood Barry, but I do know you. Despite all the grand words, you don't really love theatre.
TOM	Then why have I dedicated my whole life to flogging fridges to fucking Eskimos? # For fun?
MAGGIE	Because you love this theatre, and you loved Barry. Because Barry's in every brick of this building. That's why 'The Georgian Journey' is a blessing in disguise. # It's given you the opportunity to let go.
TOM	He'd never have let this happen. He'd have fought # them. And won. He was always so vital. In all senses.
MAGGIE	That's rubbish. He couldn't have done any more than you have. Probably less, because he wouldn't have had your inside knowledge.
TOM	What inside knowledge?
MAGGIE	That it's a lost cause.
TOM	Now that *is* rubbish.

MAGGIE   It's the truth, Tom. Inside, you know it is. I
              only hope that deep inside, you're glad it is.

              (*Pause.*)

TOM   (*much quieter now*) People were very cynical
              when we first got together. He: the seasoned
              old cynic. I: the fresh-faced innocent. You can
              imagine all the hilarious gags about sliding up
              and down Nelson's Column. But it worked. It
              did work, Mags, it # lasted. Probably

MAGGIE   I know, Tom.

TOM   because he wasn't really that cynical and I
              wasn't actually that innocent. (*Beat.*) I always
              felt Nancarrow & Nelson sounded better, but
              Barry was a stickler for billing, so Nelson &
              Nancarrow it was.

MAGGIE   Tom, you've got to let them go. Let them die
              with dignity. Why sully their reputation with
              commercial crap just to keep up with the
              Indiana Joneses?

TOM   Sometimes I do wonder, Mags, whether we
              really should be lying to all those kids. Telling
              them the streets are paved with gold; that all
              they have to do is turn again and everything'll
              be all right: fame and fortune, marriage and
              Mars bars. (*Beat. Very low key now.*) Dick
              Whittington wasn't silly, charming Jake; he
              was a grasping self-serving bastard. He never
              went to Morocco, never married Alice,
              probably never even had a fucking cat.

MAGGIE   No cat, no corporate sponsorship.

              (*Possibly they share a rather weak laugh.*)

              Let's start living for ourselves at long bloody
              last, rather than for the other bastards who
              don't give either a toss or a "thank you".

TOM   The audiences . . .

MAGGIE	No, your beloved fellow actors. # Look
TOM	What?
MAGGIE	around you, Tom. It's not a warm, cosy family. It's a snake pit. Everyone out for themselves, except us, as yet. A bunch of misfits who don't know the meaning of "community" or "society". It's only you that uses those words. Society, Tom? Norma, Robin, Wilfrid, these jokers are on the outskirts, it's the only place they can be. Oh, yeah, they're wandering minstrels, but only because no one's silly enough to let them settle next door. You've got to stop being a social worker, Tom. Theatre's a business not a charity.

(*Beat.*)

TOM	All right, forget about them; I'll think about me.
MAGGIE	Good.
TOM	(*rather haltingly*) So thinking about me, you say, "let Barry and The Old Girl go". Fine. But I've already let one of them slip away and, now, I'm scared to death that if I lose the other, I'll lose me. Without them, I don't know if I can remember who I am, Mags.
MAGGIE	(*simply*) If I don't get away from here soon, I don't know if I'll ever find out who I *could be*, Tom.

(*Beat.*)

TOM	So, up and in, it is. (*Beat.*) You all right, Mags? Meant to say it before. Look like you've been crying.
MAGGIE	Oh, I think I'm getting that bloody flu again. Can't shake it off.
TOM	Well, take care. Can't have both of us with eyes like two crows smashed into a cliff. Paul OK?

MAGGIE   Oh, fine. (*Picking up* SARAH's *wedding hat.*)
                Now get your titfer on. We're going to a
                wedding.

                (*Slow fade.*)

                (*Lights up on* BARNACLE *and* PISTACHIO,
                forestage, frontcloth.)

BARNACLE   Well, here we are, Pistachio. Outside the
                Guildhall, just in time for the weddings of Dick
                and Alice, Sarah and Alderman Fitzwarren, and
                Jack and Ulul. Ulul, that's a very funny name,
                isn't it!

PISTACHIO   It's Moroccan for Lulu. It's a very backward
                country.

BARNACLE   (*ignoring him*) And, just before the wedding,
                indeed (*Carrying the baton of the running gag
                to the last hurdle.*) at this very moment, Dick is
                inside the Guildhall being made Sir Richard
                Whittington, Lord Mayor of London. They
                should all be coming out any minute now.
                What does your watch say?

PISTACHIO   Tick tock.

BARNACLE   Sometimes I think you'd benefit from a full
                frontal lobotomy.

PISTACHIO   I'd rather have a full bottle in front of me. Nuts!

BARNACLE   Pistachio!

PISTACHIO   No, beer nuts.

BARNACLE   (*to audience*) Ah, lucky Dick! I wish there
                were something that we could all do to help him
                celebrate. But what can you give the man who
                has everything?

PISTACHIO   Penicillin.

BARNACLE   I'll do the jokes, if you don't mind.

PISTACHIO	(*to audience*) Sad. The final scene, and still labouring under the same delusion.
	(JACK *enters, yawning.*)
JACK	(*waving at audience; then at* BARNACLE *and* PISTACHIO) Hiya, kids! Hiya, Bernie and Pistachio!
BARNACLE	Ah, Jack! Just in time!
JACK	(*about to disappear again, concerned*) Oh, no, am I?
BARNACLE	(*calling him back*) No, don't go! You can help us out.
JACK	Sure. Which way did you come in?
PISTACHIO	I hope your marriage lasts to be as old as your jokes.
BARNACLE	Jack, I've just had a wonderful idea! Why don't we sing a song to celebrate Dick being made Mayor?
JACK	What a great idea! It'll help keep me awake until my wedding.
PISTACHIO	It'll also give 'em time to set the final scene up.
JACK	But, you know, Captain Barnacle, I think we're going to need some help.
BARNACLE	You're right. (*A double-take to the audience.*) Do you think they'll help?
JACK	I'm sure they would. (*To audience.*) Won't you? And, you'll never believe it, but I've just had an idea!
PISTACHIO	Well, we all make mistakes. As the hedgehog said to the scrubbing brush.

JACK	Let's split in half and have a singing competition!
BARNACLE	Yes, kids against grown-ups!
PISTACHIO	Inspired! This could set a precedent, you know.
JACK	Yes, let's see if we can make so much noise that Dick and Alice'll hear it!
PISTACHIO	(*to audience*) Do you think someone's working him with their foot?
BARNACLE	Well, the acoustics in this place are marvellous!
PISTACHIO	Pardon?
JACK	(*indicating one half of the audience*) So, all those on this side, you sing along with me.
BARNACLE	(*indicating the other half*) And all you on this side, sing along with me.
PISTACHIO	And I'll just mouth the words.
JACK	But wait! (*Indicating the audience.*) How will they know the words?
BARNACLE	Aha, I've thought of that. (*Calling up into the flies.*) Brian, lower the sheet!
PISTACHIO	(*to audience*) Well, we never saw that coming.
	(*Blackout.*)

Sunday 23rd January – the last night

The lights snap up to reveal MAGGIE *and* TOM *in the wings. The last night show is about to begin.*

MAGGIE	Well, you know my motto, Tom.
TOM	Expect the worst and accept less, # yes.
MAGGIE	Amen. The secret of true satisfaction.

Tom	Well, I've accepted the worst but I can't say I feel exactly satisfied.
Maggie	You will in time. Losing this bloody albatross'll prove the best thing that could have happened to you. Trust me.

(Norma *enters, in a bit of a state, carrying some knitting and her well-thumbed script.*)

Norma	(*as she enters*) The last night and he has to spoil it. # As if it's not
Tom	Who, Norma?
Norma	a sad occasion enough. Wilfred Raymond. Dreadful man. Should have graciously retired to an old pros' home years ago. But of course # he doesn't
Tom	What's he done now?
Norma	know the meaning of the word 'grace'.
Maggie	(*into the tannoy*) Beginners to stage, # please.
Norma	Walked past my door on the way back from the hostelry and shouted at me for knitting. Bad luck and all that superstitious twaddle. I was only doing it to calm my nerves whilst I had a quick browse of the script once more for good luck. Fair screamed at me, "You'll put a curse on us, you silly . . . " Well, I won't quote the foul-mouthed # old drunk verbatim.
Tom	Forget it, Norma. Wilf doesn't mean it. Been drifting out to sea for years. Just reached mid-Atlantic, that's all. *
Maggie	(*into tannoy*) OK, let's give 'em the one minute bell.
Norma	* Age is no excuse. I was only knitting for pity's sake. For my little niece. I used to knit

for the girls all the time when they were young.
Everything: bootees, cardies, darling little hats
with bobbles or tassels, all in the prettiest
pastel pink. They used to gurgle with sheer
joy, their little faces beaming with appreciation.
Now it's just, "Oh, Mother, don't be so
ridiculous".

(BERNIE *enters silently, and sits.* PISTACHIO
wears a muzzle.)

(*A frantic torrent*) Well, I'm not ridiculous. I
am not a silly bitch. (*Spotting* BERNIE.) Look at
him. He's the madman. Another ingrate. All
the tea I brewed! What's wrong with knitting
for one's loved ones? Even if they're not your
own. I spend my life entertaining other
people's kids. And what do I get? Hissing! I
do my best, I act, I knit, they hiss. The only
ones grateful are mine. Because I'm *here*.

TOM   (*leading her off dressing room-wards*) Come
               on, Norma. Let's go back to your room. Close
               the door and you can knit a duvet. Wilfred'll
               be none the wiser.

NORMA   (*as* TOM *leads her off*) Sheridan Morley once
               complimented me on my knitting. "Miss Bailey
               demonstrates, in the role of Bertha the maid,
               that, were we ever in any doubt, she can knit as
               well as she acts." I never dropped a stitch.

               (*They have gone.*)

MAGGIE   Unlike her new-found pal. (*Into tannoy.*) Miss
               Krabbe, your audience awaits. Would you
               kindly join them in the auditorium ready for the
               off?

               (NICK *enters under the above and begins to
               warm up rather tentatively, eyeing* PISTACHIO
               all the while. BERNIE *ignores* NICK; PISTACHIO
               *throws him the odd, very odd, glance. For a
               few seconds, there is silence, then* SUZANNE
               and JAKE *burst in from the dressing rooms.*

SUZANNE *is now dressed as a Moroccan princess.*)

JAKE	(*as he enters*) Don't walk away from me, Suzanne. # I asked you a question. What did
SUZANNE	I'm on.
MAGGIE	Yes, but round the other side. (*She exits towards the dressing rooms.*)
JAKE	you give Sally last night?
SUZANNE	A good time, which is more than you did.
JAKE	She is drugged up to the eyeballs. That's why she missed the matinée. She can barely go on # tonight.
SUZANNE	She didn't take anything she didn't want to. I was only comforting her, for Christsake, pepping her up. She needed it after being unceremoniously dumped by you.
JAKE	(*taking her to one side, and lowering his voice*) I only told her it wouldn't work. One of those things. She understood. She was fine. At least she was when I left her. Christ knows what state she was in when *you* did.
SUZANNE	(*moving stagewards*) I don't need this shit and I'm not taking it. I'm on.
	(NICK *meanwhile obviously decides that discretion is the better part of valour and exits to the dressing rooms.*)
JAKE	(*stopping* SUZANNE *exiting*) Maybe if you'd given her one more pepper-upper, you'd still be waiting to go on for her. Like you did a couple of weeks ago when Ralph Thompson was in.
SUZANNE	Who?

JAKE   The top agent who's just signed you up. It's the talk of the chorus dressing room.

(ROBIN *enters from the dressing rooms and sits with his crossword as far from* BERNIE *as possible.*)

Was it your performance as Alice he liked or the one you gave him after dinner?

(SUZANNE *slaps his face hard; he immediately grabs her wrists. A tussle.*)

SUZANNE   You silly-as-arseholes bastard. (*As she struggles free.*) I'm the only one on their way up in this lead balloon. Are you going to blame me for grabbing the only fucking parachute?

(*Beat.* SUZANNE *turns and exits onto the stage.*)

JAKE   (*as she goes*) Happy landing. (*He turns back towards the dressing rooms.*)

TOM   (*entering, passing* JAKE *on his way out*) Break a leg, Jake.

JAKE   (*as he exits*) I was thinking of a neck.

ROBIN   (*to* TOM) Ah, last night, eh, Tom?

TOM   Don't miss a trick, do you, Robin?

(*Beat; a shared chuckle perhaps.*)

ROBIN   I hate last nights. Bloody sad.

TOM   I hate get-outs. Bloody stressful. Especially with a throbber from the last night party. (*With no trace of poetry or pity.*) Tomorrow, you'll all pack up and go your separate ways. We'll tot up the books and de-rig the lanterns, rip it all down and think, "This was our Highgate Hill where Dick moved them to tears, that was the *Saucy Sal* on which we danced and sang".

ROBIN   Just think of the next one you've got to get up, love.

TOM   But it wasn't Highgate Hill, folks, it was only a sheet of canvas, and the *Saucy Sal* was simply plywood. (*Beat.*) There won't be a next one, Robin, not here.

            (*During the above,* MAGGIE *has returned and resumed her position in prompt corner.*)

MAGGIE   (*to* TOM) I hope you're not getting maudlin, Tom. Sarah's supposed to leave them with dry eyes and wet seats.

TOM   On the contrary, Mags. Once more with feeling.

MAGGIE   Good. Tonight, forget it. Tomorrow, rip it down, then launch the rest of your life with equal feeling. Tuesday, let's do lunch.

TOM   That'd be nice.

MAGGIE   It'll be business. I'm becoming an agent. I've the contacts. Just need the clients. You could be the first.

            (*Beat.*)

TOM   I'll wrap up my bundle and tie it to a stick first thing tomorrow.

ROBIN   When I was a kid, I once did 'Snow White'. Not the title role, of course. High Wycombe. Anyway, the management could only afford to pay two dwarfs, so the other five were made of hardboard. We had to keep adding lines like "Us two will scout ahead, you chaps stay here".

            (*Before anyone can respond,* WENDY *bursts in from the dressing rooms, calling out for* MAGGIE.)

WENDY   (*once she has silence*) It's Wilfred! He's
             dead. Jake just found him on the loo. *

TOM   What?

MAGGIE   * Wilfred?

ROBIN   * Who?

WENDY   (*overly patient*) Wilfred's dead.

ROBIN   He's not.

WENDY   Yes, he is.

TOM   He can't be.

WENDY   Yes, he is.

MAGGIE   No, he's not.

WENDY   Oh, yes, he fucking is. (*Beat.*) I did a First Aid
             course at Roedean. I do know.

             (*Silence.*)

ROBIN   I knew we shouldn't have spoken the last
             rhyming couplet before first night.

TOM   (*heading off; to* MAGGIE) I'll call an ambulance.
             Don't hold the house. (*To* WENDY.) Tell Darren
             he's going on as the Sultan. Then inform the
             rest of the chorus. They'll need to reblock. #
             (*To* ROBIN.) Robin, can you tell

WENDY   (*as she dashes off*) Fucking typical.

TOM   the principals. (*As he leaves.*) Let's aim for
             curtain up at 7.40.

MAGGIE   (*into tannoy*) Pete, old cock, would you play
             the overture again, we've a slight technical
             hitch back here.

ROBIN   I remember this matinée when some old girl
                   died in the audience. Probably Eastbourne.
                   Anyway, it was such a bloody quick turn-
                   around and we couldn't delay the second
                   show, so they just propped her up in the Royal
                   Box till we'd finished. (*Beat.*) I think some of
                   the evening house actually curtsied.

MAGGIE   What a way to go.

                   (*Blackout.*)

                   (QUEEN RAT *and* FAIRY BOWBELLS *are
                   discovered onstage in their traditional
                   corners; the former looks vanquished, the
                   latter victorious, with* TOMMY *by her side.*)

QUEEN RAT   Curséd be you, and your angelic retinue!

BOWBELLS   Oh, do shut up, you poor sick cretin you!
                   Let's stop this other-worldly double-act.
                   It's Christmas. A time for peace. Make a pact!

QUEEN RAT   I'd rather be the plaything for a cat!

BOWBELLS   Well, Tommy and I could soon arrange that.

                   (TOMMY *advances threateningly towards*
                   QUEEN RAT.)

QUEEN RAT   On second thoughts, you're right, I get your point.
                   (*Moving towards* FAIRY BOWBELLS *to shake her
                   hand.*)
                   Here's to an ending happy and conjoint!

BOWBELLS   To that, my fairy friend, I chime "Hear hear".

QUEEN RAT   (*to audience, stroking* TOMMY)
                   I love you all!

BOWBELLS   Don't overdo it, dear.

QUEEN RAT   (*to audience*) But just before we take our final
                                                              bow,
                   (*Pushing* TOMMY *forward.*)

My newfound buddy would like to say,

TOMMY   Meouw!

(*The three line up, facing the audience,* TOMMY
in the middle.)

BOWBELLS   And so our tale is told. Look kindly on our rhyme.
                'Tis not serious stuff; just pantomime.
                A harmless piece of sparkling, jingling folly

QUEEN RAT   To help poor mortals banish melancholy.
                To gain this end, we humble few have striven

BOWBELLS   And trust that joy and happiness we've given,

QUEEN RAT   That theatre once more has pulled off the trick.

BOWBELLS/   So farewell, kids! And "Cheerio, Dick!"
QUEEN RAT

(*Together they turn to gesture upstage, along
with* TOMMY, *as if to greet the rest of the
company.*)

(*The lights reveal the backstage area.* SALLY
is centre, sobbing hysterically, with MAGGIE
and TOM *attempting to comfort her.* ROBIN *and*
NICK *are crossing at the rear, carrying a
covered, dead body on a stretcher.* SUZANNE
and JAKE *are to one side, engaged in a furious
argument. All the while,* BERNIE *sits against
the rear wall, centre, his face an
expressionless mask.* PISTACHIO, *however, is
banging his head against the wall, violently.*)

SUZANNE   (*as a spot highlights her and* JAKE) Fuck off,
                Jake! Don't come all holier than fucking thou.
                I didn't do anything worse than you did. We
                both used # and abused her, just in different
                ways.

JAKE   What? What do you mean by that? Used and
                abused # her?

SUZANNE   The difference is I only fucked her figuratively.

                 (*At that, the lights snap out on* JAKE *and*
                 SUZANNE, *who continue to argue silently, and
                 now pick out* ROBIN *and* NICK, *carrying the
                 body.*)

ROBIN   A sad day, but inevitable. # Comes to us all.

NICK   (*to himself*) I can't handle this.

ROBIN   Always said you'd have been no good in rep,
                 love. # Not like Wilf. Change was

NICK   How would Jack handle this?

ROBIN   the name of the game. Each week a different
                 show, a different set.

NICK   I think he'd be quite idle about it all.

ROBIN   Used the same flats, just changed the order.

                 (*The lights lose* ROBIN *and* NICK, *as they
                 continue to cross the stage, and finally
                 concentrate on* SALLY, MAGGIE *and* TOM.)

SALLY   (*sobbing; almost hysterical*) I just want to go
                 home, I don't understand all this. # How can
                 you all

MAGGIE   We understand, pet.

SALLY   go on, smiling # and singing

TOM   We just do, we have to.

SALLY   after this? Bernie's gone nuts, that bitch is
                 trying to poison me, Norma's terrified of # even
                 going out

MAGGIE   I know, I know . . .

SALLY   there, Wendy's every other word is the 'c' one,
            Jake's ditched me, # and now

TOM   Shush now, Sally, come on.

SALLY   poor old Wilf's dead, and . . . and . . . how can
            you? # I don't understand. And why

TOM   We can't, not really. But we do.

SALLY   all the pussy and dick all the time? # I just
            don't understand, I just

MAGGIE   Me neither, sweetheart.

SALLY   don't understand . . .

TOM   We're actors, love.

SALLY   I want to go home.

TOM   It's called theatre.

MAGGIE   (*matter-of-fact to the last*) Just grin and hide
            it.

            (*Blackout.*)

            (*The lights snap up to reveal the entire panto
            cast, ie, all bar* MAGGIE, *on stage for their
            finalé number, possibly 'There's No Business
            Like Showbusiness'. They are all smiling,
            singing and dancing: gloriously happy and
            alive. We are saved the final applause.*)